LOVE & RESPECT

Workbook

DR. EMERSON EGGERICHS

WITH

FRITZ RIDENOUR

THOMAS NELSON
Since 1798

NASHVILLE DALLAS MEXICO CITY RIO DE JANEIRO BEIJING

Focus on the Family
Colorado Springs, Colorado

LOVE & RESPECT WORKBOOK

Published in Nashville, Tennessee. Thomas Nelson is a trademark of Thomas Nelson, Inc.

Thomas Nelson, Inc. books may be purchased in bulk for educational, business, fund-raising, or sales promotional use. For information, please e-mail SpecialMarkets@ThomasNelson.com.

Published in association with Yates and Yates, LLP, Attorneys and Literary Agents, Orange, California.

Cover Design: Charles Brock, UDG | DesignWorks, Inc.
Cover Photo: Steve Gardner, shootpw.com
Interior Design: Rainbow Graphics; Kingsport, TN.

ISBN-13: 978-1-59145-348-2
ISBN-10: 1-59145-348-8

Printed in the United States of America
07 08 09 10 11 RRD 12 11

Contents

PART TWO

THE ENERGIZING CYCLE

BEFORE YOU START YOUR STUDY OF LOVE AND RESPECT . . .

Welcome to the *Love & Respect Workbook* experience. You are about to discover and apply the single greatest secret to a successful marriage. Today, you and your mate can start fresh with the ground-breaking guidance that Dr. Emerson Eggerichs provides in this workbook and the book it accompanies—*Love & Respect*. These two books are designed to be companions, so you'll benefit most if you have a copy of the book as well as this workbook.

Based on three decades of counseling experience, as well as scientific and biblical research, the book offers you the information and tools you will need to understand what is wrong in your relationship and begin the process of correcting it. The workbook gives you and your mate a private place to complete a wide variety of exercises that are crucial to the process of making Dr. Eggerichs' breakthrough techniques a permanent part of your marriage.

Before you start your actual study, here are some helpful hints on how you can benefit most from your experience:

Come ready to let God help you work on your marriage. As you experience *Love & Respect* you will be amazed at how these two simple but powerful concepts can affect your marriage. This is no quick and easy fix, but if you are willing to spend a reasonable amount of time and effort, and make the tiniest of adjustments, this study will change you and your marriage for the better.

Study at your own pace and preference. Some of the questions are quite simple—others take more thought and effort. But as you interact with *Love & Respect* concepts, you will begin to see what Emerson is talking about. In Emerson's words, you will "get it" and once you "have it," you will never be the same.

Get acquainted with how this workbook is constructed. It covers all the *Love & Respect* book in fourteen sessions. Some sessions cover one chapter of the book, and others cover as many as three chapters. As you go through each chapter, you will note that every subhead denotes a block or section of study, and generally there is at least one question for every section. The goal is to get you involved with what Emerson is saying, to see if you agree or disagree as you apply his concepts to your marriage. When some questions deal with difficult concepts, there is extra input and explanation in the form of Emerson's Additional Commentary (see *Workbook* Appendix VI).

This workbook was designed to be used by both individuals *and* couples, so you'll notice ICONS throughout that will help you understand which questions apply to you.

First, take note that the questions *without* icons apply to *all readers*. In each chapter, be sure to answer all these questions first. Then, take note of the three types of icons used in the workbook. There are certain questions designed especially for men, while others address women only. And some of the questions should be answered as a couple. Here is a quick review:

> **Unmarked questions should be answered first in each chapter by both the man and the woman.**

 Men answer these questions.

 Women answer these questions.

 Couples answer these questions together. Answer these questions last in each chapter.

You can study this book solo. The questions are written primarily for individuals and then for couples. Therefore, if your spouse is not yet interested in *Love & Respect*, you can gain much from working alone. But as you begin putting *Love & Respect* principles into action, your spouse may decide to join you!

For maximum benefit, study with your spouse. Virtually every question has a section for spouses studying together. Remember, these questions are marked with an icon of a couple. Both of you should answer these questions together *after* you answer each question individually. As you compare and discuss your answers, you will gain new understanding of each other and how each of you sees your marriage.

Take your time. There is no hurry and no requirement to cover every last question completely. Break each session into workable parts. Concentrate on the questions that really speak to your needs as husband and wife.

Treat each other with Love and Respect. Because some of the questions probe sensitive areas, it is possible that tension will develop—even irritation and anger. Your rule should be: when dealing with sensitive issues, be sensitive to each other! If a question becomes a bit too sticky, and one of you doesn't feel up to dealing with it at the moment, table that question for possible discussion later.

Handle each other with care. As you proceed, you will soon see that a question may reflect the strength of one spouse and the vulnerability of the other. Where you are strong, or not so sensitive, your spouse is weaker and more sensitive. Where you can quickly see the need to change your attitude or something you are doing, your spouse may struggle, seeming to stubbornly hang on to habits you know have to go! By-words for your study of *love and respect* should be: patient, non-judgmental and forgiving. Always remember that God made us male and female—not wrong, just different. If both of you approach each question with compassion and empathy for each other, there will not be a critical or judgmental spirit on the part of the stronger one, and the vulnerable one will feel greater freedom to address issues and get feelings on the table.

As you study, expect God to work. To be sure, *Love & Respect* was written to put you in closer touch with your spouse. But the ultimate goal is to put you in closer touch with your Lord. Every session in this workbook includes scripture studies to guide you in times of meditation and prayer. Without prayer, your study will yield minimal returns. Pray without ceasing, and you will see God work at His pace, in His way, as He strengthens you " . . . with power through His Spirit in the inner man" (Ephesians 3:16). Love and respect each other as God loves and respects you. He will be forever pleased, and you will be forever rewarded.

Are you ready? Then let's begin!

PART ONE:
THE CRAZY CYCLE

Sessions 1 to 4 cover the Introduction and Chapters One to Seven of *Love and Respect*

A PERSONAL WORD FROM EMERSON . . .

Welcome! You are beginning a journey to love and respect, a "new" way to approach marriage that is as old as the New Testament itself. Nestled in the fifth chapter of Paul's letter to the Ephesians, hidden in plain sight, is the "secret" to controlling what I call the Crazy Cycle—and beginning to enjoy a marriage built on love for her and respect for him. Everyone who has ever been married knows what it is like to be on the Crazy Cycle: without love from him, she reacts without respect; without respect from her, he reacts without love. And so husband and wife go round and round saying and doing the same wrong and hurtful things, with seemingly no way to stop it.

As you study the first four sessions in this workbook, you will learn how the Crazy Cycle starts and why it often continues indefinitely. Most importantly, you will come to understand how to slow the Crazy Cycle and eventually bring it to a halt. I know this can happen because God empowered my wife, Sarah, and me to defeat the Crazy Cycle. He can and will empower you as well.

SESSION ONE

In preparation for this session, read the Introduction to *Love & Respect* ("Love Alone Is Not Enough") and Chapter One, "The Simple Secret to a Better Marriage." The following questions are for use in individual study or study by a husband and wife together. Remember to answer all unmarked questions first, then answer questions marked by the male or female icon (whichever applies to you). Finally, answer the questions with the couple icon, if you're studying with your mate. (Suggestions for anyone planning to use this study with a small group are in *Workbook* Appendix I, page 201.)

Questions for Chapter One

1 On page 1 of *Love & Respect*, Emerson "absolutely disagrees" with the Beatles' conclusion that "all you need is love." Emerson goes on to say that five out of ten marriages are ending in divorce because love alone is not enough. Love is vital for the wife, but what we have missed is the husband's need for respect. *Love & Respect* is all about how the wife can fulfill her need to be loved by giving her husband what he needs—respect.

Do you agree or disagree with the paragraph above? Can a wife get the love she needs simply by showing her husband respect? What if he doesn't deserve respect? Do you think Emerson is talking about conditional respect, or unconditional respect? Put down some of your thoughts here:

Compare what you wrote. Be aware that this very first question in the workbook could possibly be sensitive, so be cautious as you declare your "firm opinion." If you disagree with each other on the answers to the questions above, hold them until later in this session, when they may come up again.

2 On pages 2–4 of the book are different testimonial statements by wives who have attended a Love & Respect conference, or read Emerson's books:

"I never ever realized how important, how life-giving, respect was to my husband."

"Just a few days ago, I decided to tell my husband that I respect him. It felt so awkward to say the words, but I went for it and the reaction was unbelievable! . . . I watched his demeanor change right before my eyes."

"I wrote my husband two letters about why I respected him. I am amazed at how it has softened him in his response to me."

"I GOT IT! God granted me the power of this revelation of respecting my husband . . . [it] has changed everything . . . my approach, my response, my relationship to God and my husband."

From your point of view as a spouse, what do these statements say to you?

As a husband I think:

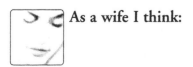
As a wife I think:

Compare your answers and talk about what you have covered so far. Some couples may find it easier to talk than others—do not force it; be sensitive to each other's feelings. Your study is just getting started, and you should have many good sharing times as you get farther into this workbook.

3 In an introduction to Part One (page 6), Emerson writes:

"I wrote this book out of desperation that was turned into inspiration. As a pastor, I counseled married couples and could not solve their problems. The major problem heard from wives was, 'He doesn't love me.' Wives are made to love, want to love and expect love. Many husbands fail to deliver. But as I kept studying Scripture and counseling couples, I finally saw the other half of the equation. Husbands weren't saying it much, but they were thinking, *She doesn't respect me.* Husbands are made to be respected, want respect, and expect respect. Many wives fail to deliver. The result is that five out of ten marriages land in divorce court (and that includes evangelical Christians).

"As I wrestled with the problem, I finally saw a connection: without love from him, she reacts without respect; without respect from her, he reacts without love. Around and around it goes. I call it the Crazy Cycle—marital craziness that has thousands of couples in its grip."

You will be learning and talking about the Crazy Cycle a lot more as this study progresses, but for now, understand that Crazy Cycles come in all shapes and sizes, as Emerson's daily mail attests. One man caught in a severe Crazy Cycle wrote:

"We were in the middle of one of our fights . . . . My wife was saying things that made me fume. She had no respect for me at all. I knew she loved me but her belligerence was too much. Fed up, I turned and went into my computer room. I left her screaming in the kitchen."

Granted, the above letter describes a marriage with the Crazy Cycle out of control. But there are other ways to be on the Crazy Cycle or to start one. Here are three more examples, based on mail Emerson has received:

A husband and wife are looking at jewelry together while shopping. The husband points excitedly and says, "Look, honey, I think those earrings are what you're looking for!" Her condescending response: "No, they aren't! Those are yellow gold and I don't like yellow gold; I want white gold!"

A wife greets her husband as he comes in from work. She wants to share what happened that day while she visited a friend. He cuts her short with: "Don't bother me. Traffic was a nightmare. I just want to kick back and watch the news until dinner."

A husband and wife have had a disagreement (the same one they usually have). She wants to talk about it; he clams up. As she badgers him to share his feelings, he picks up a newspaper and is soon engrossed in the sports page.

Choose one or more of the situations reported above. What is going on? Why could the husband feel disrespected or the wife feel unloved?

Compare notes on the examples above of how the Crazy Cycle can start up (or just keep going). If you don't seem to have a lot to discuss at this point, move on. You are just getting introduced to what the Crazy Cycle is and how it affects marriages.

4 What is your response to the term, Crazy Cycle? Does it seem to apply to your marriage—at least some of the time?

___ YES   ___ NO   ___ MAYBE

I think:

Check any of the following that apply.

I see the Crazy Cycle starting up when:

_____ a. My spouse appears unreasonable

_____ b. I appear unreasonable

_____ c. My spouse doesn't make sense

_____ d. I don't make sense

_____ e. My spouse is harsh and/or critical

_____ f. I am harsh and/or critical

_____ g. My spouse is inconsiderate

_____ h. I am inconsiderate

_____ i. We argue about sex, money, in-laws, or _____

_____ j. My spouse won't talk

_____ k. I won't talk

_____ l. My spouse talks too much

_____ m. I talk too much

_____ n. Other (describe your experience or viewpoint):

 Share your answers. Take note of what each of you has checked, but do not get into a lengthy discussion at this time. The main idea is that you both recognize how either of you could start the Crazy Cycle.

5 In 1 Corinthians 7:28 the apostle Paul writes: "Those who marry will face many troubles in this life, and I want to spare you this" (NIV). Did you ever stop to think that all married couples will have trouble? In other words, all married couples take a

spin on the Crazy Cycle from time to time. Should couples conclude they have a bad marriage simply because they sometimes have troubles and things get a bit crazy? (Additional commentary is available in *Workbook* Appendix VI.)

 Share ideas on what each of you thinks about Emerson's claim that there will always be "trouble" of some kind to deal with in marriage. It may be small, it may be huge, but trouble is something that does come up from time to time.

——————

6 In Chapter One, Emerson recounts his early life and first years of marriage as he and Sarah rode the Crazy Cycle. Reread the story of "The Jean Jacket 'Disagreement'" (pages 9–10) and analyze what Emerson learned. What was Sarah feeling? What was Emerson feeling?

Compare what you wrote down. Can either of you relate to this story? Have you had similar things happen?

7 During an argument after attending a Bible study (book pages 10–11), Emerson responds to Sarah's criticisms by saying: "Sarah, you can be right but wrong at the top of your voice." Does this statement ring a bell for you? Is your spouse ever right but wrong at the top of his/her voice? Are you ever right but wrong at the top of your voice? How does this keep the Crazy Cycle spinning?

 As you discuss this question with each other, the wisest approach is not to accuse your spouse, but to confess the times when you may have been "right but wrong at the top of your voice."

8 Read the story of "And Then I Forgot Her Birthday" (book page 12). Has something like this happened in your marriage? Did you feel unloved or disrespected? Did your spouse? Think back and describe what happened as you remember it.

Recalling a forgotten birthday may not make much difference to him, but it will to her. If a husband is the one at fault, he would do well to apologize. For more on how important birthdays and anniversaries are to wives, see Session Eight, page 115.

9 On pages 13–14 Emerson describes a pattern in his marriage of "Loving Times and Spats of Ugliness." He and Sarah love each other, but they still irritate each other in certain ways—even to this day. Can you relate to their experience? In what way?

 This is another question where you should go easy on each other. Try to identify what happens when the positive times turn negative. Are certain words said? Are certain things done or not done? Always remember the key questions: Does she feel loved? Does he feel respected?

10 In Song of Solomon 2:15, the lovers resolve to "Catch the foxes . . . the little foxes that are ruining the vineyards." In other words, they don't want anything to spoil their relationship. What are some "little foxes" that threaten to spoil your marriage and keep the Crazy Cycle rolling along?

Though we will have "trouble" in marriage (1 Corinthians 7:28), that doesn't mean we should assume trouble is always inevitable. Some trouble can be caused because we have not dealt with the "little foxes" that we know are there. What could you do to reduce some of the crazy negativity that causes unnecessary trouble? Write down some different steps you can take to drive out the "little foxes."

 Share ideas on how to go "fox hunting." Each spouse will do well to think of things he or she needs to do, not what the other spouse needs to do.

11 In "The 'Secret' Hidden in Ephesians 5:33" (book pages 14–15), Emerson explains how God helped him see the secret to defeating the Crazy Cycle. This secret is in Ephesians 5:33 (NIV):

However, each one of you also must love his wife as he loves himself,
and the wife must respect her husband.

In "How God Revealed the Love & Respect Connection" (book pages 15–17), Emerson explains how his study of Ephesians 5:33 began to show him a definite link between love and respect. He realized that a husband is to obey the command to love even if his wife does not obey the command to respect, and a wife is to obey the command to respect even if the husband does not obey the command to love. As Emerson saw it, Ephesians 5:33 didn't leave much wiggle room. A husband can't say, "I will love my wife after she respects me." Nor can a wife say, "I will respect my husband after he loves me" (see page 16). A husband's love for his wife must be unconditional, and a wife's respect for her husband must also be unconditional.

What do you think? Is there any "wiggle room" in Ephesians 5:33? Many wives believe (some with good reason) that their husbands don't deserve respect. What is Paul saying to wives who may feel like this deep down? (Additional commentary available in *Workbook* Appendix VI.)

Keep in mind each other's comfort zone. (For example, some spouses like discussing the meaning of the Greek more than others.) The key point Emerson is making is Ephesians 5:33 clearly teaches that husbands must unconditionally love their wives and wives must unconditionally respect their husbands. This can be new and striking information for a wife, so the husband should be sensitive to her need to process this idea over time.

12 For more on the concept of unconditional respect, read "Why Love & Respect Are Primary Needs" (book pages 17–19). See especially pages 18–19, which give additional comment on Ephesians 5:33 and then show how 1 Peter 3:1–2 also teaches unconditional respect for husbands. What kind of a husband is Peter talking about? How can a wife feel respect for a man who does not believe, or who is not treating her lovingly? Is she supposed to feel respect, or is Peter asking her to do something else? Write your thoughts below. (For additional interpretation of 1 Peter 3:1 and its application to husbands, see *Workbook* Appendix II.)

As you share answers, you may want to just touch on this question. To go into it in depth (see *Workbook* Appendix II) may be something you want to do at another time. The key point is that 1 Peter 3:1 is a cross-reference support to Ephesians 5:33. Both passages teach unconditional respect for the husband by the wife.

13 On page 16 of *Love & Respect*, Emerson relates that he still did not totally understand the Love & Respect Connection until God guided him to see that it is a connection that can be strained or even broken. Without love she reacts without respect, and without respect, he reacts without love—the Crazy Cycle.

Read pages 15–16 again to be sure you follow Emerson's reasoning. Does it make sense? Why or why not? How do his ideas apply to your marriage? Husband, do you think you understand how to love your wife? Wife, are you certain you understand how to respect your husband? What are some examples of how you believe you are doing this?

 I love my wife by:

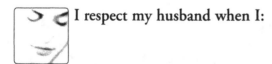 I respect my husband when I:

You can take one of two approaches on this question:

- Keep your answer to yourself at this point and use it as your personal checkpoint on how you are treating your spouse.

- Share your answer with your spouse and get his or her feedback. Try to give each other positive suggestions and encouragement whenever possible.

14 On page 20, Emerson describes and illustrates the "life-changing decision" he and Sarah have both made. He has decided to believe that no matter what Sarah says or does, she does not have evil intentions. She might have a nasty or peevish moment but deep in her heart she intends to do good. She may come across in a way that seems disrespectful to Emerson, but that is not her real purpose. And Sarah has decided to believe that, no matter what Emerson says or does, he does not intend, deep in his heart, ill will toward her. He may come across in an angry way, and give her a cold stare that seems unloving, but his real purpose is not to be uncaring. (See his accounts on pages 20–22 of the book concerning peppered eggs and wet towels to see how this plays out in their marriage.)

Take a few minutes to end your study of Session One by thinking and praying about a woman's deep need for love and a man's deep need for respect. Consider how the decision Emerson describes on page 20 of the book applies to you. If you are studying alone, you may be in one of several situations: You may be trying to find answers for your marriage, but your spouse isn't interested in studying anything with you at this point. You would like to decide that no matter what your spouse says or does, deep down your spouse loves (or respects) you, but you aren't quite sure this is always true. In fact, at this point you may be thinking you need more time and more study of how love and respect work in a marriage. Emerson has many more insights to share, beginning with Session Two, which covers why men and women are so different, and which often causes communication problems.

Talk about what this chapter has been saying to both of you. Share any "light bulb moments," questions, or concerns you may have. Perhaps you are ready to make the same decision about each other's good intentions that Emerson and Sarah have made (see book page 20). Perhaps one of you isn't quite ready. Wives, in particular, if your husband seems unwilling or uncomfortable about taking this step so early in your study together, do not be critical or disrespectful. Do not rush something like this. Be willing to pray and think about it. Both of you may need more time, or more information about the Crazy Cycle and why people can't seem to slow it down. As Emerson says, there is much more he wants to tell you. In Session Two he will talk about how husbands and wives can learn to communicate, despite their differences as men and women.

A JOURNAL OF MY JOURNEY
TO LOVE & RESPECT

Every session will conclude with Emerson's meditations on foundational Scripture passages cited in *Love & Respect*. The space provided below for you to interact with his observations will allow you to create a personal journal of your journey to love and respect. By the time you finish this workbook, you'll have a permanent record of your growth and development as an individual or as a couple.

SCRIPTURE MEDITATIONS

1. "Enjoy life with the woman whom you love" (Ecclesiastes 9:9). When on the Crazy Cycle, many a husband wants to throw up his hands in defeat. Does Ecclesiastes 9:9 suggest that a husband could influence the emotional temperature of his marriage more than he might think? As a husband, what might you do for or with your wife in the next several hours that is wholesome and enjoyable—something to ignite a smile in both of you?

2. The Crazy Cycle is, indeed, "the evil of folly and the foolishness of madness" (Ecclesiastes 7:25). When the Bible speaks of "madness," it does not refer to someone who is mentally deranged. This person has a sound mind, but he or she is acting or reacting in ways that God deems foolish, unfruitful, even "crazy." Think about it: how crazy is it for a husband to react in unloving ways when feeling disrespected? How crazy is it for a wife to react in disrespectful ways when feeling unloved? You might say, "But it's natural to react sometimes in an unloving or disrespectful way." Natural, yes, but effective, no. What do unloving or disrespectful reactions do to the spirit of a spouse?

3. In Ephesians 5:33, Paul writes: "Each one of you also must love his wife as he loves himself, and the wife must respect her husband" (NIV). Because Ephesians 5 contains what is considered the greatest treatise in the Bible on marriage, it is safe to say that Ephesians 5:33 is, in effect, God's "last word" to us on this subject. But God's last word on marriage won't help you if it isn't heard. Do you believe that if, as a couple, you apply love and respect to your marriage you will experience marriage in the way God intended? Do you believe love and respect will guide the two of you in responding correctly to troubles that are bound to come to your marriage? Do you believe that at the end of your life, after living out love and respect, you will be able to pray: "Thank You, Lord, for showing me Your simple plan for marriage"? (Put down your honest thoughts here. If you have any doubts write them out, then give them to God in prayer.)

My current thoughts about our marriage:

SESSION TWO

In preparation for this session, read Chapter Two in *Love & Respect*, "To Communicate, Decipher the Code." The following questions are for use in individual study, or study by a husband and wife together. Remember to answer all unmarked questions first, then answer questions marked by the male or female icon (whichever applies to you). Finally, answer the questions with the couple icon, if you're studying with your mate. (Suggestions for using this workbook with a group are in *Workbook* Appendix I, page 201.)

Questions for Chapter Two

1 On page 25, Emerson opens Chapter Two by asserting that husbands and wives communicate in "code" and must learn how to decipher the messages they send each other. What do you think?

How often does your spouse seem to communicate in a "code" that is hard to decipher or understand?

CONSTANTLY ___   OFTEN ___   NOW AND THEN ___   SELDOM ___

Discuss this question gently and sensitively, particularly if your answers fall in the "constantly" or "often" range. If you do have a communication problem, this session is designed to get you talking about it and learning how to work on it. Guard against getting into an argument about "who communicates the worst."

2 Read the story of the "Tenth Anniversary Card" that turned out to be a birthday card (book pages 25–27.) When the wife responded in anger, what coded message was she sending to her husband? What coded message was he sending to his wife when he responded defensively by saying, "I made an honest mistake; give me a break"? How did they start the evening anticipating a wonderful tenth anniversary and wind up on the Crazy Cycle?

 Compare notes with your spouse (and with Emerson's additional commentary on Question 7 found in *Workbook* Appendix VI). Talk about how the couple wound up on the Crazy Cycle on a night when they should have been celebrating.

3 Read the story that starts under the heading, "All You Want Me for Is Sex!" (book pages 27–29). What message was the wife sending in code as she reeled off a barrage of problems, appointments, and assignments the minute her husband returned from his trip? What message was the husband sending in code when he said sarcastically, "Great to see you after a week"?

4 Later, when this same husband and wife go to bed after their exhausting day, what coded messages do they send each other? What mistakes do they make in doing so? Why can't either spouse decipher the other's code? How did they get on the Crazy Cycle?

Compare your answers to Questions 3 and 4. If you aren't sure you have identified the encoded messages correctly, hold them for discussion in Question 7, where Emerson will review this story and make comments on what the encoded messages meant.

5 Under "Craziness—Just Keep Flipping the Light Switch" (book page 29), Emerson compares the Crazy Cycle to mindlessly flipping a light switch over and over when the light won't come on. Instead of figuring out the problem, you just keep flipping that switch. Emerson's point is simple: "Craziness happens when we keep doing the same things over and over with the same ill effect." What things do you or your spouse do over and over that help start you both on the Crazy Cycle?

Go easy with each other when discussing this question. Confess your faults, not your spouse's. Try to have some fun with this, and don't call each other "crazy." The truth is, any couple can get on the Crazy Cycle together, and you must work together to slow it down and stop it.

———

6 In "Why Do Couples Communicate in Code?" (book page 30), Emerson paraphrases a well-known explanation of why and how we send messages in code and don't communicate: "What I say is not what you hear, and what you think you heard is not what I meant at all." Read the story about Emerson and Sarah almost getting into a serious argument about who was listening to what on the radio. How did Emerson finally break the codes they were sending and stop the problem from escalating?

 You can learn a lot about communicating as you discuss your answers to this question. The way Emerson stopped the Crazy Cycle from spinning was to realize he was not being clear (and not very loving either). Once he broke the pattern of miscommunication, he and Sarah were able to understand each other and prevent sparks from becoming a fire.

———

7 Read the section titled, "When the Issue Isn't the Issue" (book pages 31–32). What was the real issue when the husband gave the wife the wrong kind of greeting card?

What was the real issue as the businessman's wife turned him down when he wanted sex?

Compare your answers. Did you agree that the real issue in these stories, as it usually is in all marital arguments or fights, is love and respect? She doesn't feel loved or she desperately needs a kiss or a hug—something to assure her she is loved. And he doesn't feel respected. He needs to feel he is appreciated and that he is someone his wife looks up to, not down upon. For interpretation of the encoded messages the spouses were sending each other in each story, see additional commentary on Question 7 in *Workbook* Appendix VI.

Are you beginning to see the importance of "decoding" each other when one or both of you sounds irritated, angry, or sarcastic? No spouse can decode his or her mate perfectly, but it is vital to understand that the need to decode is always there, and the more you both work on doing it, the better your communication will be.

8 In "We're as Different as Pink and Blue" (book pages 32–35), how is male-female communication described? According to Emerson, women see the world through _____ sunglasses and hear with _____ hearing aids. Men see the world through _____ sunglasses and hear with _____ hearing aids. Why is it important to understand these differences? How could understanding their pink and blue perspectives have helped the couple whose tenth anniversary was spoiled by the wrong kind of greeting card or the couple who reconnected so badly after his week on the road?

Compare your answers, as well as your respective understandings of the pink and blue analogy. This question is really a continuation of Question 7. Obviously, the pink and blue perspectives of the wife and husband have everything to do with the kinds of codes they send and the decoding that needs to be done. Try working together to re-create each story to make it come out with a happy ending, or at least with the Crazy Cycle slowing down and even stopping. In either story, what might the husband have said or done that would have felt more loving to the wife? What might the wife have said or done that would have felt more respectful to the husband?

9 Emerson constantly receives letters from spouses who finally "get it" concerning the deep need in wives for love and the deep need in husbands for respect. Following is one such letter, from a wife, who came to see clearly the difference between "pink" and "blue":

I read your book this week and I have been convicted. I have always felt that if I just loved my husband enough, he would come around and be the kind of man my father was. Then God proceeded to show me the many ways I have been disrespectful towards my husband— and my father!

I now see that most of the arguments have been started by me, in my misunderstanding of the way my husband thinks. I have been arrogant and self-righteous in my misguided attempts at communication in hopes of bringing us together. What a fool I've been! It sounds so dumb when I write it down!

I wrote him a letter today in apology and my desire to change. He called to say, "It's okay, it was nothing!" What a man!

I never saw my disrespect as disobedience to Christ before. That really hurt. I know now what a grievous sin it is and I pray for grace and help to change. Thank you for this liberating truth.

Grace and peace to you and may I see and hear in blue!

What has this wife understood? What does she mean when she says: "... may I hear and see in blue!"?

Here's another letter, from a husband who also finally "got it." He and his wife had started going to a counselor before they attended a Love & Respect Conference, and they continued to go afterward as they tried to apply love and respect principles. He writes:

Recently, I had forgotten to do something for my wife. She expressed hurt and anger toward me at the next [counseling] session. Our counselor concluded that I have not been "hearing" her because I react in a "defensive" way to her comments, and this has hurt her and caused her to shut down. He has challenged me to learn her "language" [pink] so that I will "hear" her. Subsequently, she will melt and then respond with respect. . . .

I accept my divine command to unconditionally love my wife through any technique that works. I still do fall into the Crazy Cycle, but I try my best to stay off of it. I do intend to sign up for "pink language lessons."

What has this husband understood? What does he mean when he says he wants to "sign up for 'pink language' lessons"?

You may wish to discuss one or both of these letters at length. In each case the spouse writing the letter has gotten the point: "pink" and "blue" must try to see and hear in the other color. When pink or blue sees it only one way, the Crazy Cycle will keep on spinning. If both spouses are agreed, now would be a good time to pledge to each other respectively:

As a wife, I want to see and hear in blue a lot more.

As a husband, I want to see and hear in pink a lot more.

10 What does Emerson mean near the bottom of book page 34 when he sums up the wrong anniversary card debacle by saying: ". . . and so two essentially good-willed people wound up spinning on the Crazy Cycle with no clue about how to slow it down or stop it"? How does he define *good-willed* on the top of page 35? Put his definition in your own words beginning with: "My spouse . . ."

Compare your definitions of *good-willed.* This term will be popping up again and again in this study. The key point to remember is that no matter how nasty, irritating, or unreasonable your good-willed spouse is, he or she does not mean to hurt you in the ultimate, long-range sense. Oh, there may be some intent to hurt on a short-range basis, but this is not what your spouse really wants. What every spouse wants is love for her and respect for him. (For more on the concept of "good will" and questions like: "How can a sinful person have good will?" go to http://loveandrespect.com/pearl/.)

---

11 In "Scientific Research Confirms the Centrality of Love & Respect" (book pages 35–37), read the conclusions of marriage research expert John Gottman, who studied two thousand couples who had been married twenty to forty years to the same partner. What single factor stood out as a reason they stayed together for the long term?

   ___ a. having enough money

   ___ b. attending church regularly

   ___ c. a loving, respectful tone to their conversations

   ___ d. spending enough time together

Gottman adds that contempt is "perhaps the most corrosive force in marriage." Do you think he is right?

 Compare your answers. Talk about how contempt can hurt and how a loving, respectful tone can heal.

12 Read the analogy described under "You're Stepping on My Air Hose!" (book pages 37–38). Emerson pictures the wife with an air hose leading to a big tank labeled "Love." What happens when the husband does something to "step on her air hose"?

Which of the following statements are examples of how a husband can step on his wife's air hose?

____ a. "I'll do the dishes, honey. You had a rough day with the kids."

____ b. "Can't you get that kid to be quiet? I'm trying to get a few minutes rest."

____ c. "I know we planned to spend some time tonight talking, but the guys want to come over to play cards."

____ d. "Sorry I couldn't call sooner. The meeting ran late, but I should be home about 6:30."

Compare your answers. These choices should be "no brainers" for both of you, but use this question to get into your own discussion of how a husband can step on his wife's air hose. (Try not to step on each other's air hose as you talk together.)

13 On book pages 37–38, Emerson continues his illustration by picturing the husband with an air hose leading to a big tank labeled "Respect." What happens if his wife happens to "step on his air hose"?

Which of the following statements are examples of how a wife can step on her husband's air hose?

   ___ a "The bills keep piling up. Why can't you bring in more money?"

   ___ b. "Honey, I know things are tight, and I'm so thankful that you get out there every day, working hard to make a way for us."

   ___ c. "Jane's husband doesn't lie around watching so much TV."

   ___ d. "I'm so grateful you like being home and being available when I need help."

 You should find the right choices fairly easy to identify, but use the question to get into a discussion of what happens in your home. How can you step on each other's air hose, perhaps in all innocence?

---

14 In "Men Hear Criticism as Contempt; Women Feel Silence as Hostility" (book pages 38–40), Emerson gives valuable insight on just how pink and blue sunglasses and hearing aids can affect a marriage. List at least three statements or phrases that stand out for you, from your pink or blue point of view.

   1.

   2.

   3.

Compare notes on what you find. Note that Emerson observes that spouses may have good will (they intend no evil toward each other), but because they don't decipher each other's code, she sees only his failure to love and he sees only her failure to respect. They lash out and the Crazy Cycle continues to spin! Talk about how to decipher each other's codes, how to slow and stop the Crazy Cycle. (For more ideas, see *Love & Respect* Appendix A, pages 305–7.)

15 The following is a letter from a wife who describes her life with her husband on the Crazy Cycle. As you read it, make notes on the following: Who is stepping on whose air hose and why? What starts this Crazy Cycle? What keeps it going?

We have been married for a long time . . . . We have difficult and challenging jobs and he feels that if I want to discuss something with him, somehow I think I know more than he does. I have never been a shrinking violet and the thing my husband hates about me is what my boss loves about me. I can be very aggressive and I get things done. Should I keep my mouth shut? It's getting worse because we don't seem to be able to come to any kind of agreement, which is distressing at the very least. I am losing hope because we don't ever seem to get anywhere. I try to talk and he stonewalls me; he tries to talk and I stonewall him. It goes nowhere.

My notes:

Talk about what you have noted in the letter above. How does the wife's "Type A Personality" step on her husband's air hose? What is his basic way of fighting back that steps on her air hose? What does their "he stonewalls me, I stonewall him" routine tell you about this couple?

16 On book page 40 Emerson gives the secret to at least start decoding your spouse's messages: "Whenever a wife is complaining, criticizing, or crying, she is sending her encoded message: 'I want your love!' And whenever a husband is speaking harshly or sometimes not speaking at all, he is sending his encoded message: 'I want your respect.'"

 How well do you decode your wife's complaints? Though not all of her complaints are cries for love (she can just be having a "bad hair day"), it helps to think first that her complaint might be rooted in her cry for love. Describe a time when you heard her cry for love underneath her complaint and responded lovingly. (If you can't think of any, just write your thoughts about how willing you are to listen better and decode her complaints.)

To complete this exercise, fill in the following: "The next time my wife complains or criticizes I will show her love by . . ."

How well do you decode your husband's actions or words when he needs respect? Silence or harshness are not always cries for respect, but they can be. Sometimes pride, or the inability to verbalize his need for respect can keep the need covered. Never forget that his "Respect Tank" is there and that you could be stepping on his air hose. Can you think of any times recently when you heard his cry for respect underneath his silence or harshness? (If you can't, just write your honest thoughts about how willing you are to decode his behavior and try to show respect.)

To complete this exercise, fill in the following: "The next time my husband appears unloving or harsh, I will show him respect by . . ."

Go slowly as you compare what you have written. This could be sensitive, but the benefits are well worth it. One area to explore is how the messages one spouse is sending another could be misread. For example, when a wife complains or criticizes, it's possible that she is frustrated about something unknown to the husband. She is not necessarily feeling a husband's lack of love. Of course, it still doesn't hurt if a husband reaches out with a touch or a hug to say, "It's okay, I'm still here for you." On the other hand, a husband's lack of love can also be hard to read. Sometimes the "big, dumb buck" is not looking for respect; he's just being selfish, unaware, or ignorant of how to treat his wife. A good approach for both husbands and wives is in *Love & Respect* Appendix A, under "To communicate feelings . . ." (book page 306). Spouses should never say, "You're being unloving," or "You're being disrespectful." As calmly as possible, she can say, "That felt unloving," or he can say, "That felt disrespectful." Then go on from there as explained on page 306.

17 As you complete your personal study of Session Two, take some time to think and pray about the messages you may be sending your spouse in code (and vice versa). And as you pray, ask yourself some basic questions: when I see the spirit of my spouse deflating, do I understand that the issue is never the real issue, which is a lack of love and respect? Do I grasp the importance of "pink" and "blue"—how different my mate and I are? Am I fully aware of my "air hose" and how it can be stepped on? Am I fully aware of how I might be stepping on my spouse's "air hose"?

If necessary, review book pages 31–35 and pages 37–40. These ideas are simply put, but they are profound. How well you embrace and practice them will have everything to do with how well you play your part in stopping, or at least slowing, the Crazy Cycle.

Talk about what this chapter has been saying to both of you. Share any "light bulb moments," questions, or differing perceptions. Write down how well each of you responds to the following principles or concepts in this chapter (use a scale of 1–10, with 10 meaning "totally get it," as one way to measure your responses):

____ The issue at hand may not be the real issue.

____ Pink and Blue are very different.

____ Each of us has an air hose that can be stepped on by the other.

___ Her complaints can mean, "Please come across more lovingly!"

___ His withdrawal can mean, "Please come across more respectfully!"

Although Emerson's word pictures (pink and blue, air hose) are playful, they contain vital and practical truths. The better you understand and actually practice them, the better you will communicate with each other. Be aware that it may sound simple, but it is not. In Session Three, based on Chapters Three and Four of the book, Emerson will explain why.

A JOURNAL OF MY JOURNEY
TO LOVE AND RESPECT

As part of your journal, every session includes a study of foundational scripture passages quoted in the margins or text of the book. As you interact with Emerson's meditations below, make notes as part of your journal. There is additional space at the end to record your current thoughts about your marriage and the progress you hope to make with this study.

SCRIPTURE MEDITATIONS

1. When counseling couples I often quote to them James 4:1: "What causes fights and quarrels among you?" (NIV). I point out that the apostle James wants each of us to evaluate why he or she is having conflicts—particularly if we are married. James continues: "You want something, but don't get it" (James 4:2 NIV). What happens when a spouse does not get love or respect? As a wife, if you feel unloved, what do you do to try to get your husband's love? Do any of these words or actions sometimes lead to quarrels? As a husband, if you feel disrespected, what do you do to get your wife's respect? Do unloving words or actions (or just stonewalling her) help? Evaluate what you have been doing to this point while on the Crazy Cycle. How effective is fighting and quarreling to get what you want?

2. Runaway divorce statistics reveal that ". . . insanity is in their hearts . . ." (Ecclesiastes 9:3). As a wife, when you do disrespectful things in a misguided attempt to motivate your husband's love, has it ever occurred to you that this is a little bit crazy? How often each week do you go a bit "insane" in an effort to get your husband to love you more? As a husband, when you do unloving things to make your wife respect you more, does it ever occur to you, "I am acting a little nuts here"? How many times this past week did you say to yourself (consciously or unconsciously), "I am not going to show love to that woman until she starts respecting me more"? If you both continue with this sort of "insanity," how likely is it that you could be pushing your marriage over the edge? How long will it be before you become a divorce statistic?

3. What can happen when a husband tries to obey a command from God's heart? In Ephesians 5:33, Paul is not making a mere suggestion when he writes, ". . . each one of you also must love his wife as he loves himself" (NIV). A husband who took this verse seriously wrote to tell me, "The information God gave you is working all over in my life. I have seen the glow in [my wife's] eyes when I apply it and the defeat [and] the despair . . . when I fail to practice the principles you are trying to teach me through your material and God's word." Husband, what is Ephesians 5:33a for you? A command? Or a "suggestion"? Wife, read Ephesians 5:33b, which tells you to respect your

husband. For you, is this a clear command, or a suggestion you can follow if he "earns" your respect?

My current thoughts about our marriage:

SESSION THREE

In preparation for this session, read Chapter Three, "Why She Won't Respect; Why He Won't Love" and Chapter Four, "What Men Fear Most Will Keep the Crazy Cycle Spinning." The following questions are for individual study, or study by husband and wife together. Remember to answer all unmarked questions first, then answer questions marked by the male or female icon (whichever applies to you). Finally, answer the questions with the couple icon, if you're studying with your mate. (Suggestions for anyone planning to use this study with a small group can be found in *Workbook* Appendix I, page 201.)

Questions for Chapter Three

So far you have been introduced to the Love and Respect Connection and the Crazy Cycle. You have learned about "pink" and "blue" and differences between men and women. You know how to be more careful about stepping on your spouse's air hose. You understand the dynamics of how the Crazy Cycle can affect a marriage: When she feels unloved, she can react in ways that feel disrespectful to him. When he feels disrespected, he can react in ways that feel unloving to her. And around and around they go. Nobody wants to be on the Crazy Cycle, even for a short time. Some couples, unfortunately, have been on it for years. Getting off and staying off is not as easy as you might think. In the two chapters of *Love & Respect* covered in this session, you will dig a little deeper into why wives find it hard to respect and why husbands in turn won't love.

1 No one has ever expressed the Crazy Cycle dilemma better than the husband whose letter appears on pages 41–42 of *Love & Respect*. Read his letter carefully. What do you hear him saying from deep within his soul? What is his wife saying about him and their marriage? What do you think it does to this man to hear, "You're not the man I thought you were"?

Compare notes on how you think a husband might feel when told, "You're not the man I thought you were." Then, to add a "fair and balanced" tone to your discussion, also consider this question: "What do you think it does to a woman when her husband angrily delivers his own message, which blames her for their problems?"

2 Read "Unconditional Respect—An Oxymoron?" (book pages 42–44). In his many years of counseling, Emerson has often heard women say they have never heard the two words "unconditional respect" put together in the context of a relationship (page 43). To these women unconditional respect sounds like an oxymoron (a term created by putting together two words that appear to be incongruous or contradictory). Why do you think so many women feel this way? Choose from the following ideas, or write your own:

____ a. They think respect is something a husband has to earn.

____ b. They think husbands are so unloving, they don't deserve respect.

____ c. They think that giving a husband unconditional respect is giving him license to do anything he wants.

____ d. I think:

Discuss the answers you chose above. You may also want to tackle questions like the following: why does telling a husband he has to earn his wife's respect put him in a lose-lose situation? What is the difference between showing respect and feeling respect? Is it okay for a wife to show respect, even though she doesn't feel respect? What do facial expressions and tone of voice have to do with how a wife shows her husband unconditional respect?

3 In "It All Goes Back to Pink and Blue" (book page 45), a wife is quoted: "We think so differently, I don't even relate to what he considers respect (or the lack of it)." How could this wife adjust her pink sunglasses and pink hearing aids so she might begin to understand her husband's need for respect? Would it help if she remembered her husband's need for respect is just as great as her need for love? At the same time, how could this woman's husband adjust his blue sunglasses and hearing aids? How crucial is it that he respond patiently to his wife's struggle with the new idea of "unconditional respect" for him, especially if he has done things that deeply hurt her? Write your thoughts here and on the next page:

Talk about your respective perceptions of "respect." What positive things could happen if each of you made a slight adjustment?

———

4 Continuing on book page 45, Emerson admits that for years as a pastor he went along with the cultural emphasis on unconditional love by the husband for the wife as the key to a good marriage. When he switched his message and started giving equal weight to unconditional respect for husbands, he got a mixed reception. One women's group actually fired him after he taught two sessions! They wanted someone to speak on "How to Love Your Husband." What they failed to see was that the way for a wife to fully love her husband is to respect him in ways that are meaningful to him. What do you think this might entail? How can a woman respect her husband in meaningful ways? When a wife attempts to show this kind of respect, what can a husband do in response to show his appreciation? Put your thoughts in writing:

Share what you have written. If either or both of you are struggling a bit with the concept of a man's deep need for respect, be sensitive to each other. It also might help to use some of the suggestions under "Things to say to lighten up the relationship," *Love & Respect* Appendix A, page 307.

5 In "Respect Is a Man's Deepest Value" (book pages 49–52), Emerson reports on a national survey in which 400 men were asked which they could endure better: (a) to be left alone and unloved in the world, or (b) to feel inadequate and disrespected by everyone. Seventy-four percent said they would prefer being left alone and unloved over feeling inadequate and disrespected (see page 49).

Would you have been among the 74 percent who believed the more negative experience would be feeling inadequate and disrespected? Why or why not?

 Do the results of this survey question surprise you? Why or why not?

Compare your answers and also talk about Emerson's analogy (bottom of book page 49) in which he compares love and respect to food and water. Do you agree with his statement, "For men, love is like food, and respect is like water"? If love is like food (important) and respect is like water (even more important), what does this suggest for your marriage?

6 Emerson is often asked if there is any passage in Scripture where men are instructed to respect their wives as well as love them. Under "Husbands Are to Value Wives as Equals" (book pages 52–54), he cites 1 Peter 3:7, where Peter tells the husband to show his wife honor as ". . . a fellow heir of the grace of life." How does Emerson interpret this phrase (see last paragraph, page 52)? How does Galatians 3:28 teach the same idea?

Discuss the concept that although husband and wife are very different, as male and female they are equal in the eyes of God (see Galatians 3:28). How might a husband appear to forget this equality and unintentionally come across to his wife in a condescending manner? What does his wife feel during such moments? What practical things can a husband do to show he values his wife as his equal?

7 On book page 53 Emerson develops the concept that women are to be first in importance, while men are to be first among equals. As you think about how comfortable you are with these "firsts," consider these questions:

 Do you think your wife longs to be first in importance because she is a prima donna or because she wants to respond, give, and serve?

Do most husbands want to be seen as first among equals because they believe it is their "right" to dominate, or because they believe it is their responsibility to lead, protect, and even die for their family?

Compare your answers. In the second paragraph, book page 54, Emerson states: "When he honors her as first in importance and she respects him as first among equals, their marriage works." Do you think he is right? Are you willing to make this a major goal in your marriage? Is your spouse?

8 Under "Husbands: Do Not Say, 'I Told You So!'" (book page 54), Emerson cautions husbands that the concept of unconditional respect can be a "huge piece of information" for a wife to process. Why should a husband *never* say, "I told you so!" or try to use unconditional respect as a weapon?

Talk about what each of you is thinking and feeling. Obviously, a wise husband will not "rub it in" if his wife is struggling to process what Scripture teaches. Also read together on book page 55 the two letters from husbands after they attended a Love and Respect Conference. What insights did each man receive, and how did this information affect his attitude toward his wife?

Questions for Chapter Four

9 As he starts Chapter Four on page 57 of the book, Emerson discusses a powerful factor that can keep the Crazy Cycle spinning: the male fear of criticism, and especially contempt. Men may look powerful and impervious to their wives' words, but underneath they are very vulnerable. The male species is often labeled as the one that likes to get into fights, and as Emerson pointed out in Chapter Three, it is the male who primarily responds to the call to war, to protect home and family. Nonetheless, males do not handle conflict with their wives well at all when they feel disrespected (see survey questions results, page 58). Emerson writes: "Men know deep down that their wives love them, but they are not at all sure that their wives respect them." Are men being overly sensitive or perhaps a bit arrogant by being so concerned about being respected? Write down what you honestly think:

Share what you wrote with each other. Also read together Emerson's idea that among men there is an "honor code"—from boyhood men learn there are certain things men just don't say to one another. A woman will talk to a husband in the home in a way that a man would never talk to him. "He can't believe she can be so belligerent, so disrespectful" (bottom of book page 59). Does your experience as a husband bear this out? As a wife, do you think you ever talk to your husband in a "belligerent" manner?

10 Read "Are You a Criticizer or a Stonewaller?" (book pages 60–61), then answer these questions: Who is the criticizer and who is the stonewaller in your marriage? Why do men (as a rule) stonewall their wives?

 This can be a delicate question for a husband and wife to discuss, so go easy on each other. Be sure you both define *stonewalling* the same way. Simply put, stonewalling is refusing to talk, period.

11 On book pages 61–62, "How Women Deal with Conflict Between Themselves" describes a typical female approach to conflict with another female, like a best girlfriend. Why do a wife's complaints and criticisms, expressed during conflicts with her husband, seldom result in shared sorrow, hugs, and even laughter as often happens with a best girlfriend? Choose from one of the ideas below, then add your own thoughts:

____ a. Husbands are too proud to admit they are wrong.

____ b. Husbands don't see their wives' deeper goal of reconciliation.

____ c. Husbands clam up because ongoing criticism feels like contempt.

____ d. Wives are more critical and judgmental of their husbands than of their girlfriends.

____ e. I think:

Share your answers. How do your perceptions differ? Do you see examples of "pink" (her viewpoint) and "blue" (his viewpoint)? Why is it obviously not a good idea for a wife to deal with her husband in the same way she deals with a best girlfriend?

—

12 In "A Wife's Self-Image May Depend on Her Husband's Approval" (book pages 62–63), read the letter from the wife who realizes that negative confrontation (being way too demanding and critical of her husband) doesn't work. As you analyze her confession of mistakes, what would you suggest that might work much better?

 Compare your findings on the wife's letter. Discussing this question can be a real opportunity to work together positively to understand how Love and Respect principles apply to your marriage. Can both of you fill in the Crazy Cycle maxim below, without going to the diagram on page 5 of *Love & Respect*?

Without _____ she reacts without _____.

and

Without _____ he reacts without _____.

—

13 Read "A Wife's Scolding Can Start the Crazy Cycle" (book pages 63–66). Why do wives often make the innocent mistake of scolding (or mothering) their husbands?

Talk about any "scolding" that might be going on in your marriage. Husband, be gentle in describing what you might think is scolding. Wife, try not to be defensive if he labels what you think are "constructive comments" as scolding. How can the male need for unconditional respect cause him to interpret certain comments by his wife as "scolding"? (For ideas on what the wife can do, see Question 14 below.)

14 To avoid sounding like she is scolding, which of the following questions is the best one for a wife to ask herself as she interacts with her husband?

_____ a. Is what I am about to say/do going to let him know that we are equals and he cannot treat me as "lesser than"?

_____ b. Is what I am about to say/do going to come across as loving or unloving?

_____ c. Is what I am about to say/do going to come across as respectful or disrespectful?

Talk about which response on the previous page is the best question for a wife to ask. Then identify the best question for a husband to ask himself before interacting with his wife. (See *Love & Respect* Appendix A, page 305, under "Always Ask Yourself." Also go over the "Taboos" on page 307.)

15 On book page 66 is an account of how one woman asked her husband: "Do you want me to tell you I love you or respect you?" What was his answer?

 At this point in the study, are you comfortable with asking your husband this same question? YES___ NO___ NOT SURE____

 What would be your answer? LOVE____ RESPECT_____

 If you feel comfortable doing so, share your answers and feelings. If a husband answers "Respect," he should try to help his wife understand without shaming her. Put a "U" next to any statements below that would help a wife Understand and a "D" next to any statements that would put her on the defensive.

___ The reason I am so unloving is because you are so disrespectful.

___ I'm sure you love me, but I don't always have assurance you respect me.

___ I know you don't intend to be disrespectful, but sometimes you come across as disrespectful. At those moments I know I should love you anyway, but I don't know how and it's safer to stonewall.

___ If you would just meet my need for respect, this marriage would be great.

___ I couldn't care less about your love; just give me respect.

___ I know you often feel I don't deserve respect, and you're right. But I need you to respect who I am deep down, even though on the surface I'm somebody neither one of us likes at times.

16 In "So That's It . . . I Need Respect!" (book pages 67–69), analyze the letter on page 68 from a wife whose husband strayed into an affair. Without excusing the husband's wrongdoing, what were some reasons he strayed? What do these reasons suggest about ways to respect a husband?

Discuss the contents of the letter. As a wife you may be tempted to dismiss its many valuable tips because an adulteress is described as using her wiles to seduce the husband. This would be a mistake. What is wrong with seeing your husband as handsome, witty, and intelligent? Obviously all this can be overdone, but there are suggestions here for how a wife can respect her husband and give his ego a respectful, but not phony, boost. At the same time, there is a warning here for both spouses. A wife may not be tempted in the same way her husband can be tempted, but she is vulnerable nonetheless. The wise husband pays attention to his wife's vulnerabilities and never ignores or belittles them. Many a wife has been drawn into an affair because she felt lonely and unloved. The best way to protect your marriage from an affair is love and respect—love for her, respect for him.

17 Read the section, "All This Should Be Obvious, Right?" (book pages 69–71). How true does the following statement at the very bottom of page 69 sound to you: "We easily see what is done to us before we see what we are doing to our mate"?

VERY TRUE ___   SOMEWHAT TRUE___   NOT TRUE AT ALL ___

Does this saying remind you of any scripture passages (see Matthew 7:12; Luke 6:31)? Why do husbands and wives often find it hardest to practice the Golden Rule with each other?

Talk about what it means for a Love and Respect couple to practice the "Love and Respect Golden Rule": the wife should respect her husband as she wants to be loved; the husband should love his wife as he wants to be respected. Why is practicing this particular rule difficult? How can you help each other do it more consistently? (For some good review, see Chapter Two in *Love & Respect*.)

18 On book page 71 Emerson states that he believes married couples are at a cross-roads. Then he asks some penetrating questions. These questions appear below, restated to apply directly to you and your spouse:

Will you appreciate your husband's need for respect, or will you denounce his feelings? Will you discover that the best way to love a husband is by respecting him in ways that are meaningful to him? Or will you focus on what you might feel is the key to a happy marriage—your womanly feelings—and dismiss his needs as antiquated chauvinism or male arrogance?

Will you appreciate your wife's need for love or just continue to ignore her feelings? Will you discover the best way to love your wife is to look beyond her criticisms and complaints to see why she isn't feeling loved? Or will you just cower before her apparent contempt and retreat to the shelter of your "stone wall?"

Spend some time in prayer as you answer these questions. It may be that you and your spouse are at the crossroads Emerson mentions. Will you take the fork labeled "Love and Respect?" Read the letter from the wife who, together with her husband, took that fork (book page 72). At this point in your study, are you gaining confidence that the simple message of *Love & Respect* really can work? Why or why not?

 The many questions above can be heavy for both of you to deal with, but they can pay off handsomely in slowing and stopping the Crazy Cycle. Be honest, but sensitive to each other and share from the heart.

19 On book page 72, Emerson closes the chapter by admitting that at times he may sound like he is hammering wives for their lack of unconditional respect for their husbands. He continues: "But I'm not trying to hammer wives—I'm trying to help them, because I know how pivotal the wife's respect can be in slowing down the Crazy Cycle. Yes, many men are unloving clods to one degree or another, but they can change. In fact, many of them want to change, and the best way to get them to change is treating them with unconditional respect."

Respond to the above paragraph from your point of view as a wife or a husband. Do you think Emerson is trying to help wives, not hammer them?

YES ___   NO ___   NOT COMPLETELY SURE, NEED TO KNOW MORE ___

I think . . .

 Give this question some careful thought and discussion. Husband, if your wife is still feeling a little "hammered" even after reading Emerson's assurances that he is really trying to help, listen to what she is saying and do not simply say things like, "You're foolish to worry," or, worse, "You may feel hammered, but it's what you needed to hear." Tell her that you want to be a more loving husband, and her respect can do nothing but help you achieve that goal.

20 As you complete this session, it may be a good time to review Question 18 and the answers you gave. Are you truly ready to take the fork in the road labeled "Love and Respect"? Write down your honest feelings at this point:

 You may feel the need to go over the heavy questions in Question 18 and talk about them a little more. Go slowly with this. Be sensitive to each other and honor any doubts or questions either of you may have. You may want to go back over Question 19 as well. Wives need understanding as they process what unconditional respect means to them and how they should act toward their husbands. Even though Emerson assures wives he is trying to help, not hammer, them, they may still feel a bit sensitive. Pray together about your study so far and your marriage. The Crazy Cycle is not easily slowed or stopped. It can be hard work, so let God help.

A JOURNAL OF MY JOURNEY TO LOVE AND RESPECT

Continue creating your own journal by interacting with the following scriptures cited in *Love & Respect*. You may wish to make notes as you interact with Emerson's meditations. There is additional space to write your current thoughts about your marriage and your study so far.

SCRIPTURE MEDITATIONS

1. In 1 Peter 3:1–2 Peter instructs wives to be submissive (give respect) to their husbands, even if they do not believe or obey God's Word and are undeserving of respect. If a wife does this, Peter writes, her husband may be won over as he observes her "respectful behavior." What does Peter mean by "respectful behavior" on the part of a wife before her husband? I believe that part of what Peter had in mind includes a wife's tone of voice and facial expression. When he isn't the man she wants him to be (loving and considerate), can she still show him unconditional respect with the way she talks and the look on her face? She is not asked to endorse his unloving actions; she is asked to show him unconditional respect, just as he is supposed to show her unconditional love. Difficult? Very. But it can work wonders. As Peter implies, it is less about what a wife says (verbal language) and far more about how she comes across (nonverbal language). A good-willed husband, no matter how badly he might be fouling things up at the moment, will find it hard to continue resisting unconditional respect.

2. Why is it that Scripture instructs men to "fight for your . . . wives" (Nehemiah 4:14), but women are never instructed to fight for their husbands? On the pages of any piece of well-known literature, does the prince see himself as the rescuer of the princess, or does the princess want the prince to depend on her for protection? If an

intruder enters a home, what will the wife think if Harry screams, "Sally! Protect me! Go get that mean man out of here so I can stop huddling in the corner!"? What does a husband feel when his wife never respectfully acknowledges and praises his desire to protect her? Question for her: "Does my husband have a need to be respected (looked up to) in a way that I have been overlooking?"

3. In a marriage especially, "Reckless words pierce like a sword . . ." (Proverbs 12:18 NIV). How deep is the wound if a husband snarls in anger, "Nobody could ever love you!"? How deeply does it cut when a wife retorts: "Nobody could ever respect you!"? Neither spouse "means it" but the effect is like a sword thrust, nonetheless. The Love and Respect couple works hard at never using "reckless" words, and instead heeds the rest of Proverbs 12:18: ". . . the tongue of the wise brings healing" (NIV).

4. A good passage for any married couple is Proverbs 14:8: "The wisdom of the prudent is to give thought to their ways . . ." (NIV). As you reflect on your study of *Love & Respect* so far, have you given much thought to your "ways"? As a husband, when you feel disrespected, is your way of reacting loving or unloving? As a wife, when you feel unloved, is your way of reacting respectful or disrespectful? It is so very easy to rationalize that your way of reacting is solely the fault of your mate and to tell yourself, "If my spouse changed, all would be well." Take the rest of Proverbs 14:8 as the Lord's warning: ". . . but the folly of fools is deception" (NIV). In other words, fools deceive themselves.

My current thoughts about our marriage:

SESSION FOUR

This session is the last in Part One: The Crazy Cycle. Session Four covers Chapters Five, Six, and Seven of the *Love & Respect* book and deals with some of the most frequently voiced issues raised by the thousands of couples Emerson has helped slow or stop the Crazy Cycle. In preparation for this session, read Chapters Five through Seven of *Love & Respect.* As you read, you may identify with many of the questions and concerns others have voiced. You may prefer to concentrate on only one or two of the chapters, or you may find all three helpful. Choose what fits your situation. It is possible that none of these chapters will seem to fit your experience exactly. We suggest you go over them anyway, using the questions in Session Four as a review of key issues and principles that affect this marriage. Remember to answer all unmarked questions first, then answer questions marked by the male or female icon (whichever applies to you). Finally, answer the questions with the couple icon, if you're studying with your mate. (Suggestions for anyone planning to use this study with a small group can be found in *Workbook* Appendix I, page 201.)

Questions for Chapter Five

1 In the opening paragraph of Chapter Five (book page 73), Emerson relates that during many years of counseling couples, he has observed that old Crazy Cycle habits are hard to break. She may want to change, but "the rat needs to earn my respect" attitude dies hard. He would like to be different, but he fears looking like an unloving fool—again. As you begin this session, where are you on this continuum?

Do you have any fears of being a "doormat" if you really try to respect your husband unconditionally? Write your honest thoughts here:

Do you have any fears of looking like a fool if you try to unconditionally love your wife and fail—or she doesn't respond with respect? Write your honest thoughts here:

One (or both) of you may feel a little uncomfortable discussing your answer(s) to the questions above. Admitting your fears and then talking about them can be beneficial, but only if both of you are willing to share your hearts.

2 The concerns described in Question 1 raise another major question that spouses have. Read "Who Should Make the First Move?" (book pages 74–75) carefully. What is Emerson's answer to spouses who wonder: "Should I make the first move?"

Why does Emerson claim that the spouse who makes the first move can rarely lose?

This is another question that you may feel reluctant to discuss. Even so, being willing to discuss this is, in a sense, being willing to make the first move! If one of you is willing to take the risk, the rewards will be well worth it.

3 In "Not a Doormat but a Woman with Power" (book pages 75–77), Emerson attempts to assure wives he is not a chauvinist in disguise, trying to lure them into a life of subservience. Read this material carefully, then go down the "list of a wife's fears" below and check off anything that you believe is a concern in your marriage.

Which of the following fears concerns you to some degree at this time?

___ If I respect him, he won't really be more loving.

___ If I respect him, I will wind up a doormat, and doing whatever he wants.

___ If I respect him, I'll have to bury my brains, never think for myself or speak my mind.

___ If I respect him, he will ignore how I hurt and where I'm vulnerable.

___ If I respect him, he'll become arrogant and self-centered.

___ If I respect him, I'll have to do something I don't really feel, and that's impossible.

___ My fear, in my own words, is:

Do you see anything in the above list that may be of concern to your wife? Check those concerns and be ready to talk about them.

This question provides plenty of opportunity for sensitive sharing. Wife, if you don't have any of these fears, you should tell your husband, which will be a big encouragement to him. Husband, if your wife does have fears about showing you unconditional respect, you can do several things: First, be thankful that she is courageous and humble enough to tell you. Second, remember she is a good-willed woman who wants your love. Third, do not dismiss her fears as "silly" or just say, "Oh, you don't have to worry about that." Fourth, seek to understand her and empathize as much as possible.

4 According to "Not a Doormat but a Woman with Power" (book pages 75–77), one of the ways a wife feels empowered is when she corrects or "mothers" her husband (page 76). According to Emerson's counsel, why doesn't this work? Finish his observation on page 77: when a wife continues to mother, correct, or goad a husband into changing, she wins the battle but loses ____ _____.

This question is similar to Questions 13 and 14 in Session 3, which dealt with the wife's scolding. If you choose to discuss this one, be careful of stepping on each other's air hose. If the two of you can share without arguing, it will be helpful for him to explain when he feels he is being "corrected and mothered," and for her to learn how she can come across a bit differently as she constantly sees things that need putting right. Remember, if you can avoid battling each other, and see each other as an ally, not an enemy, you will win the war of the Crazy Cycle.

5 In "What If You're Afraid to Take the Risk?" (book pages 77–80), there are several letters from wives who were hesitant to try showing their husbands respect—but who trusted God anyway. Read these letters carefully. Write out phrases that may give you help, hope, or assurance for your marriage.

Husbands, while this question is designed primarily for wives, you can benefit from answering it as well and then comparing notes with your wife. Can you identify with why the husbands described in these letters were so energized? As you share with your wife, what can you say to her to alleviate any fears or questions she may still have? Whatever you do, refrain from shaming your wife as she awakens to your need for respect.

6 In "Husbands, Remember Only One Idea—Love" (book pages 80–82), Emerson admits that there have been plenty of times when he has felt like the husband who wrote in to say: "I have spent the last twenty years literally consumed with trying to figure out what is going on in our marriage." What has helped Emerson during those times? What are the two questions a husband must focus on when his wife gets critical or negative? (See book page 81.)

Even though Question 6 is directed primarily toward the husband, the wife can benefit by answering it as well and then comparing her answers to her husband's. As a wife, do you agree that when you get critical or angry you are actually saying, in one way or another, "I need your love, please love me!"? As a husband, are you remembering to ask yourself: "Will what I do or say next come across as loving or unloving?" Ask your wife how she thinks you are doing in that department.

7 Read the story of how "This Husband Decoded in Jail" (book pages 82–85). As he spent the entire weekend in jail, this man had an "epiphany experience" that helped him to finally understand his wife's angry messages. What stands out in this story from your point of view as a spouse?

Compare your answers, which may be quite different. Concerning this man's story, Emerson says: "Husbands and wives please note: physical violence against a wife is reprehensible and evil. Sharing this man's letter should not be construed as sanctioning such evil in any way. The story shows what can happen when God works in a husband's life and he learns how to decode his wife."

8 Two more letters from husbands who learned to decode their wives are on book pages 85–86. As you read these letters, make notes on some important ways a spouse can decode. What phrases or ideas stand out? Which ones should you use more often?

Compare your answers. How are all of these ideas about decoding summed up in Emerson's observation, "The Crazy Cycle can be slowed—and stopped —if only we would have eyes to see and ears to hear"? Not only is it important for you to "get it" (understand what you need to do), it is also very important to listen and respond when your mate "gets it" as well. (See Emerson's additional comments on Question 8 in *Workbook* Appendix VI.)

Questions for Chapter Six

9 Chapter Six opens with a letter from a woman who was trying to respect her alcoholic husband, but she did not "want to be a hypocrite." How does Emerson answer this concern (book pages 87–88)? Why does continuing with criticism and anger only mean that a wife shoots herself in both feet?

This could be a delicate question, especially if the wife has any feelings about being a hypocrite as she tries to show the husband unconditional respect. Go slowly and gently and remember that practicing Love and Respect isn't about feelings; it's about doing what the Scriptures teach.

10 On book page 89 Emerson tells of having asked a wife: "Are you afraid that your respectful manner will lessen your chances of motivating your husband to change?" Read her response, then write your own. According to Emerson, "Obeying God's Word does not make a wife a powerless hypocrite." Do you agree? Explain.

Husband, while this question is directed to your wife, write your answer as well, then discuss it with her. As your wife shows you respect, especially when you are not as loving as you could be, do you see her as "power-less" or "power-full"? Why?

11 Read the letter from a wife at the bottom of book page 90, plus the paragraph at the top of page 91. What did she get out of being respectful? What has she made sure to do in response to all his loving acts? How do you think the husband feels when he comes home to a clean house, a hot meal, and a wife who looks good and acts like she is happy to see him?

You and your mate may see this question as rather simple, not to mention that it flies in the face of a culture where a stay-at-home-spouse is unrealistic in many households. Nonetheless, there are principles here any couple can apply. Today's woman expects her emotional needs to be met, even if she has a career, because her traditional need for love has not changed. Conversely, a husband has a traditional need for respect, but when he expresses it, some want to tar and feather him. If the way your spouse wants to be treated seems unrealistic or outdated, look beyond all the cultural baggage and see the deeper need to be loved or respected. Talk about why the Love and Respect Connection is so simple, yet sometimes so difficult. Why can it be so powerful when used by two good-willed people?

12 Read "Refuse to Play Rodney Dangerfield—Don't Stonewall!" (book pages 91–92). Instead of muttering, "I just don't get no respect," husbands are to move toward their wives even when they are receiving "verbal deathblows." How does Proverbs 12:16 help a husband when his wife is being abusively disrespectful?

Handle this question (and each other) with care. As a husband, you have the opportunity to apologize for the times you "stonewalled" your wife when you received what felt like "verbal deathblows" from her when she felt angry (and unloved). Tell her that from now on you want to follow Proverbs 12:16 and "conceal the dishonor." In other words, no stonewalling—no getting angry in return. You just want to keep coming with unconditional love. As a wife, you have the opportunity to apologize for your anger and promise to give your husband unconditional respect. Both of you realize you can't be perfect at practicing Love and Respect, but you also know that just being willing to try means real progress. Pray together for guidance as you seek to slow and stop the Crazy Cycle.

13 In "I Used to Say, 'I'll Show Her!'" (book pages 92–94), Emerson confesses how he reacted badly to Sarah when feeling disrespected. Then he discovered a way to motivate her to be more respectful, which in turn motivated him to be more loving! Read this section carefully and find the combination of short sentences Emerson used to develop what amounts to the "Love and Respect 'I' Message." Also turn to *Love & Respect* Appendix A, page 306, "To communicate feelings or start discussion," where an example is given for the wife as well as the husband. To start memorizing the "Love and Respect 'I' Message," fill in the blanks below:

As a husband, you can say: "That felt _____. Did I just come across as _____?"

As a wife, you can say: "That felt _____. Did I just come across as

_____?"

Note on book page 306 what you are to say if your spouse answers yes to your question. Is the "Love and Respect 'I' Message" something you can use in your marriage? Write your thoughts:

 Compare your answers and also discuss what Emerson and Sarah have done when angry, which is stated in Ephesians 4:26 (see "It Works—Even on Our Bad Days," book page 94). Read this verse together. Could this verse change the way you deal with anger?

14 In "If I Can Do It, So Can You" (book pages 95–97), there are two letters from struggling husbands (bottom of page 95, top of page 96). Finish this bit of advice Emerson gives both of them: "Gentlemen, it is true you are not designed by God to enjoy contempt, but He does call you to _____ _____ _____."

As you talk together, note the comments by marriage researcher John Gottman who concluded it is more effective for a husband to embrace his wife's anger (bottom of book page 96). (For more discussion ideas, see Emerson's additional comments in *Workbook* Appendix VI.)

15 At the bottom of book page 96, top of 97, Emerson suggests what a husband can say if his wife vents her feelings with venomous remarks: "Honey, I love you. I don't want this. When you talk this way, I know you're feeling unloved. Let's work on

this. I want to come across more lovingly, and I hope you would like to come across more respectfully."

 Because a husband does not love naturally, God commands him to do so (see Ephesians 5:25–33). It may never feel "natural" to say something like what is quoted above, when your wife is venting her anger at you, but as a man of honor, are you willing to try it?

YES ___   NO ___   NOT SURE ___

 If your husband used Emerson's suggestions when you were venting your anger at him, how might this make you feel? Would it help? Why or why not?

Compare your answers. Is Emerson's suggestion for turning aside a wife's anger something that could work in your marriage right now? Talk about how it would feel in the middle of an argument or angry exchange for the husband to talk about wanting to be more loving and hoping the wife could be more respectful. (For more ideas on defusing anger, see "Things to Remember," *Love & Respect* Appendix A, pages 305–6.)

---

16 Read the story of "The Husband Who Never Stopped Loving" (book pages 97–99). Note two or three things that stand out for you in the wife's letter about how her husband wouldn't give up on her, even when it seemed hopeless.

Compare notes, then talk and pray about your own marriage. Emerson adds this note on the value of prayer: "As you go through this study of *Love & Respect*, you may have moments of feeling overwhelmed. All husbands and wives who are believers in Christ have His promise: 'Come to Me, all who are weary and heavy-laden, and I will give you rest' (Matthew 11:28). And Peter adds: '[cast] all your anxiety on Him, because He cares for you' (1 Peter 5:7). If you are feeling weary and heavy-laden, will you pray to the Father? Will you cast your anxieties on Him? Do this because He cares for you. Jesus, the Perfect One, depended on the Father while on earth. All God's children are free to do the same. Depend on God for all your needs. He is eager to help you!"

17 Read carefully the second paragraph on book page 99 (beginning, "No matter how desperate or hopeless a marriage may seem . . ."). What do you think? Can love and respect, plus basic goodwill in both spouses, conquer anything?

I TOTALLY AGREE _____   I PARTIALLY AGREE _____   I DOUBT IT _____

My comments:

 You may know people who face tremendous problems in their marriage such as adultery, abuse, or addictions. You may face tremendous problems yourself. Does Love and Respect work when the going gets really tough? (Those who may need specific help to deal with adultery, spousal abuse, and drug addictions, go to the following Web site: http://www.loveandrespect.com/pearl.)

Questions for Chapter Seven

18 As he has counseled wives over the years, Emerson often hears comments like these: "Forgive him? Yes, I know what Jesus said about seventy times seven, and I've forgiven him at least that many times! But when is he going to ask me for forgiveness? When is he ever going to care about how much he hurts me?" Is there some truth in comments like these? Shouldn't a husband ask for forgiveness in order to be forgiven? Can granting forgiveness, even when it isn't wanted, really help the situation at all? Read the opening book pages of Chapter Seven (101–3). Then put down your response to Emerson's teaching:

Talk about what it means to forgive. Do you agree with Emerson's assertion that when you forgive someone for being unloving, you give up your right to hold a grudge? Note the letter from the wife on page 103. What insights does she provide that might make forgiveness possible, even if it doesn't seem practical? Husbands, don't skip this material because it seems to be directed to wives. You may need to do some forgiving yourself, or perhaps it is time you asked for forgiveness. Forgiving someone, or being forgiven, can be a humbling experience. Each of you should try to be sensitive to the other's needs at this time.

19 At the bottom of book page 105, Emerson writes, "Nothing is easier than judging, nothing is harder than forgiving, and nothing can reap more blessings." Read the letters from the wife whose husband strayed into adultery (pages 104–5). How did she find it in her heart to forgive him? What was her driving motivation?

Compare notes on what you see in this woman's letters. She faced having to decide to forgive her husband at the hardest level: for his immorality. It may be of help to spend time together reading and discussing Emerson's views on forgiveness at two levels (see *Workbook* Appendix III, page 207). He gives sound biblical advice to the spouse who has been wounded deep in the heart by a mate's adultery. For the woman who wrote the letters, her strongest motivation was, obviously, her faith and trust in God. She had no trust for her husband, and little or no inclination to forgive. But when she did, he responded. Emerson adds: "Situations like this do not always have such a happy ending, but God calls us to obey Him and His word, one step at a time, and to accept what happens as His will."

20 Read book page 106, "If You Fail to Love Her, Rebound," then respond to the following:

 How good a rebounder are you? (In other words, how well do you bounce back when you are unloving and get clobbered with contempt?)

 How good a rebounder is your husband when you criticize him with good reason? (For that matter, how good a rebounder are you when he reacts to your disrespect?)

Talk together about Emerson's "rebound" analogy. Even if you know nothing about basketball, the principle is there to use: a good rebounder is determined to try again and again. Do one or both of you need to be a better rebounder?

21 Read Emerson's humorous account of how he has had to rebound after blowing it with Sarah (bottom of book page 106 to top of 109). What truths in his transparent admissions stand out for you?

As a husband, note especially the two choices you have if your wife comes at you "with disrespect flashing in her eyes and venom shooting from her tongue": defend your pride or surrender with unconditional love. As a wife, how would you respond if your husband said, "I'm sorry. I know I've been unloving"?

22 In "Marriage—A Two-Become-One Proposition" (book pages 109–12), Emerson claims that when couples practice love and respect, "Bad marriages become good, boring marriages become exciting, and good marriages become better." Note these words from a husband who from all appearances had a good marriage (and even conducted marriage seminars with his wife): "On a scale of 1–10 we were living with a 5–6 marriage most of the time." When he and his wife started making Love and Respect a priority, that number went way up. How would you rate your marriage right now on a scale of 1–10, with 10 being "great"? Our marriage is a _____.

 Be aware that this question could be difficult to discuss. Be sensitive to each other and willing to hear the other person's reasons for the number he/she chose. Concentrate on agreeing about how you can work together to make that number higher.

---

23 In "From the Crazy Cycle to the Energizing Cycle" (book pages 112–13), Emerson reminds spouses that you can slow or stop the Crazy Cycle, but you can never get off completely. He and Sarah know they have to work continually at controlling the Crazy Cycle, and some of the best ways they have learned to do this are stated in capsule form in *Love & Respect* Appendix A, especially in "Always Ask Yourself" and "Things to Remember" (pages 305–6). Take time to go over these suggestions now, and write down several ideas that stand out as things you want to practice as you move into Part II—The Energizing Cycle.

 As you complete your study of Part I: The Crazy Cycle, share and pray together concerning these questions:

1. How much progress have we made in slowing and stopping the Crazy Cycle?

2. What can we do, as a couple, to keep the Crazy Cycle under control?

A JOURNAL OF MY JOURNEY
TO LOVE AND RESPECT

This section of your workbook is your private area to write whatever you are thinking or feeling at this time. The Scripture Meditations can help you start thinking and praying and putting down what is on your heart. There is also room to record any other current thoughts about your marriage.

SCRIPTURE MEDITATIONS

1. In your marriage, be the first to "seek peace and pursue it" (1 Peter 3:11). Can you say you are the one in your marriage who consistently seeks peace and pursues it? Do you ever seek peace at any price, ignoring or compromising the clear teaching of Scripture? Or, do you stubbornly and selfishly demand your own way in small matters because you foolishly make these "little things" symbols of how you are unloved or disrespected? Consider this wife's letter: "I turned the temperature down last year . . . [then] my husband bought a plastic box that fits over the dial complete with lock and key. . . . I was appalled when he put a locked box over the temperature dial. . . . I found a way to change the dial without using the key [and] I turned the heat down to 68. This has always been an area where we don't agree. He told me last month that he felt I was being disrespectful." How would you answer this wife? At this rate, why will she and her husband not experience peace? How could they change in an attempt to seek peace?

2. It is always wise for a husband to be "humble in spirit" (1 Peter 3:8). What does it mean for a husband to be humble in spirit? Will a wife walk all over a husband who approaches her in this way?

3. Over the years, as I have blown it and been unloving to Sarah, I have found solace in Proverbs 24:16: "Though a righteous man falls seven times, he rises again"(NIV). The husband who tries to live an honorable life with his wife, but fails, knows two things: (1) He is "righteous" only through the blood of Christ; (2) he can no more always show his wife perfect love than she can show him perfect respect. What does Proverbs 24:16 tell the husband or wife to do in the moment of failure? The last time you came across as unloving or disrespectful what did you do?

4. To stop the Crazy Cycle, and keep it in its cage, seek to obey God's Word "which also performs its work in you who believe" (1 Thessalonians 2:13). We have God's promise that His Word will do His work deep in our souls! Your marriage isn't first about performance; it's about God doing a work in and through you: ". . . for it is God who is at work in you, both to will and to work for His good pleasure" (Philippians 2:13). As you live with your spouse, stop at least once each day and pray, "Dear God, perform Your work in me. Do Your work through me. Please, Lord, I need You!"

My current thoughts about our marriage:

PART TWO:
THE ENERGIZING CYCLE

Sessions 5 to 12 cover Chapters Eight to Twenty-Two of *Love & Respect*

A PERSONAL WORD FROM EMERSON:

I hope you have made progress to this point in slowing or stopping the effects of the Crazy Cycle on your marriage. Your next step is to learn how to keep the Crazy Cycle from spinning, or how to stop it if it seems to be starting up again. You can do this by getting on the Energizing Cycle in which his love motivates her respect and her respect motivates his love.

To help you get on the Energizing Cycle and stay there, I developed two acronyms covering six important principles for each spouse. The acronym C-O-U-P-L-E contains advice for husbands in six brief chapters on Closeness, Openness, Understanding, Peacemaking, Loyalty, and Esteem. The acronym C-H-A-I-R-S contains advice for wives in six brief chapters on Conquest, Hierarchy, Authority, Insight, Relationship, and Sexuality.

Keep in mind that if you are studying together with your spouse, discussing some of these questions may be tough going. Husbands and wives need to be sensitive to each other and take it slowly, easily, and gently. There is no rule that says you must exhaustively discuss every question. Some questions may prove sticky, even irritating to one or both of you. The first rule in being a Love and Respect couple is to do just that—show love and respect to each other! This will mean not always saying everything that may be on your mind. Be honest, but not brutally honest. (Speak the truth in love—Ephesians 4:15.) Remember, having a difference of opinion or a different understanding of something does not mean you have major problems as a couple. What you must guard against, however, is allowing disagreements to turn into disapproval of the other person. Always, the goal is Love and Respect, whether you agree or disagree. The husband should focus on loving his wife, the wife on respecting her husband. If you do this, the Energizing Cycle will hum along nicely and the Crazy Cycle will not have a chance to spin.

SESSION FIVE

In preparation for this session, read the first two chapters in Part Two of *Love & Respect*, which covers the Energizing Cycle. Begin with Chapter Eight, "C-O-U-P-L-E: How to Spell Love to Your Wife," and Chapter Nine, "Closeness—She Wants You to Be Close." The following questions are for individual study or study by a couple. Remember to answer all unmarked questions first, then answer questions marked by the male or female icon (whichever applies to you). Finally, answer the questions with the couple icon, if you're studying with your mate. (Suggestions for leading a small group can be found in *Workbook* Appendix I, page 201.)

This session opens your study of C-O-U-P-L-E, six important principles that will help a husband learn important aspects of loving his wife. In Love and Respect, just under the title of Chapter 8, is a brief note to wives saying the next several chapters are for "husbands only, but wives are invited to read along." Wives are also invited to study along in Sessions 5-8 of this workbook, so please do! As your husband discusses the six parts of C-O-U-P-L-E with you, he will learn more about how to love you (and you will learn how to help him do it better!).

A SPECIAL WORD FOR HUSBANDS FROM EMERSON:

Welcome to the Energizing Cycle and your study of the acronym C-O-U-P-L-E: Closeness, Openness, Understanding, Peacemaking, Loyalty, Esteem. These are the six principles you can practice to make your wife feel loved. More than that, you can use C-O-U-P-L-E as a diagnostic tool to tell when you and your wife are slipping off the Energizing Cycle and back on the Crazy Cycle. According to the Crazy Cycle, a wife acts disrespectfully when she isn't feeling loved. Her disrespect is not justified, but when it does happen you can say to yourself, "Since my wife is reacting in ways that feel disrespectful to me, there is a good chance I have done something to make her feel unloved. I have two choices: react to her unlovingly, or try to decode. Which one of the principles in C-O-U-P-L-E might I be neglecting in her view?" This way you soften your reaction, as you remember that your wife is basically a good-willed woman who is not intending to show you contempt.

Next, depending on the situation (what has been going on between the two of you), you can probably make a good guess at what's wrong. For example, you've been working long hours, and she is feeling the need for closeness. Talk to her and ask if this is what is wrong. If she says it is, you can say you are sorry for your behavior, make adjustments, and get the Energizing Cycle going again.

But what do you do if, for whatever reason, you can't decode (figure out what is bothering her)? If that happens, you can communicate your feelings to your wife by gently (not defensively or aggressively) saying, "I'm feeling disrespected right now. Have I been coming across as unloving? How can I come across more lovingly?" (In other words, tell me where I am messing things up.)

I believe that as you go through C-O-U-P-L-E for husbands and C-H-A-I-R-S for wives, you will get to know each other better than you ever have before as you are challenged, stretched, and, I hope, blessed. But remember, if any of the questions in the following sessions makes either of you uncomfortable, agree together to table that item for right now. Later, you may be ready to come back and discuss the topic with real profit as you go to new levels of Love and Respect. But for now, let's get going with the Energizing Cycle—and have a great trip!

Questions for Chapter Eight

1 To get started with Session Five, the six words represented by C-O-U-P-L-E are listed below. Next to each word is a brief definition. Under each word, write what it suggests to you. Does your definition match the one given?

Closeness: She wants you to be close.

 My definition:

Openness: She wants you to open up to her.

 My definition:

Understanding: Don't try to "fix" her; just listen.

 My definition:

Peacemaking: She wants you to say, "I'm sorry."

 My definition:

Loyalty: She needs to know you're committed.

 My definition:

Esteem: She wants you to honor and cherish her.

 My definition:

Which of these six principles sounds most interesting? Which is most necessary to a happy marriage? Why?

Husbands and wives should compare their respective definitions and discuss them. How did they differ from the definitions given? How does your definition differ from your spouse's? How do your answers to the other two questions differ? When your study of C-O-U-P-L-E is complete, see if your opinions have changed and note why they might have changed

2 On book page 118, Emerson defines the acrostic word C-O-U-P-L-E as "two people connected together." What does it mean to you to be "connected" to your spouse?

This question could prove sensitive, especially if the husband sees his wife's efforts to connect with him as an effort to control him. Go over book page 118 again. Wife, do you agree that when you come across as negative and offensive you are really crying out for C-O-U-P-L-E, the things your husband can do to connect with you? Husband, can you see yourself starting to decode your wife's messages, which may sound negative, but are really her cries for your love?

3 Farther down on page 118 Emerson writes, "Wives want connectivity. . . . Women confront to connect." Why is this good? How can it turn out "not so good"?

Discuss your answers and learn a little more about one another.

4 In "This Husband Wouldn't Believe Me Until . . ." (book pages 118–20) is a story about a husband who saw his wife's effort to connect by confronting as an effort to control him. He finally "got it" and realized this was not true, but only after attending a Love and Respect Conference. Why do many men fear being controlled? How could understanding this fear help prevent the Crazy Cycle from spinning? Who needs to understand it more—the husband or the wife?

Generally speaking, men want to be responsibly in control. See especially Session Ten, under C-H-A-I-R-S, which talks about the wife respecting the husband's desire to protect, provide, serve, and lead. All of these involve being responsibly in control to one degree or another. When a husband feels his role in any of these areas is threatened, he may start to think his wife is trying to control him. ("She's trying to mother me.") On the other hand, if a wife feels her husband is being too dictatorial or demanding, she will feel unloved. ("He treats me like a doormat!") Talk together about the issue of control. Wife, let your husband know you are not trying to "wear the pants"; you only wish to connect with him. Husband, ask your wife for honest feedback about how "controlling" you are in your marriage. A good-willed husband wants to be a loving and responsible servant-leader. Talk about how the husband's control can be good as long as a wife feels secure, but bad if she starts to feel unloved. Perhaps the key phrase is "responsible servant-leader." What does that look and feel like to each of you?

5 Read carefully the "Learn to Trust Your Instruments" section on pages 120–21. How can practicing C-O-U-P-L-E prevent "marital vertigo?" Husbands, are you willing to "trust your instrument panel"?

NO PROBLEM ___   NOT TOTALLY SURE ___   DOUBTFUL ___

Husband, discuss your answer with your wife and share any doubts you may have about how well you can practice the principles in C-O-U-P-L-E (that is, "trust your instrument panel"). For example, are you willing to ask her if she confronts you to connect or control? (In other words, does she want to connect to create mutual understanding or is she confronting to control you and get her way?) Many wives are also mothers (or want to be), and it is in their nature to be helpful. Not only that, but wives are called to be "helpers" (Genesis 2:18). Can a wife seek to help her husband and come across as controlling without meaning to? Should the husband be willing to trust her goodwill, even though her helping can make him feel like she is being "bossy" at times?

---

6 In "In the Ocean of Conflict, Men Sink Unless . . ." (book pages 121–22), Emerson shares the story of one husband who had the guts not to stonewall his angry wife. How would you describe what he did as he "trusted his instrument panel"?

 Compare your answers, which could be very revealing by showing how each of you think. Also see *Love & Respect* Appendix C (page 311), which lists "need communicator" statements both of you can use when appropriate.

---

7 At the bottom of book page 122, as he summarizes Chapter Eight, Emerson writes, "To turn to your wife in the middle of a conflict and say, 'I am sorry, will you forgive me?' takes guts. I know because I have been there. It isn't pleasant, but it works powerfully. Over time it becomes easier, but it is never natural. Even so, this response gives you the power to drain negativity out of your wife in conflict after conflict." Why does it take guts to say "I'm sorry"? What often stands in a husband's way?

This can be a good question to discuss, but only if both of you are "up for it." Be sensitive to each other's needs and, if feasible, talk together about why it's hard for him to say, "I'm sorry." Is it pride? Or is it fear that later she will use his apology against him in a disrespectful way?

Questions for Chapter Nine

8 Chapter Nine opens with a biblical definition of *closeness* (book page 125). Write that definition below and be sure to add what it means "to cleave." Obviously "cleaving" involves sex, but what other kinds of closeness are involved?

 Talk together about what closeness means to each of you. How important is it for the husband to let his wife know he wants to be close with a look, a touch, or a smile?

9 Read carefully "The First Few Seconds Set the Tone" (book pages 126–27). Why are those moments when a couple comes together after being apart all day so important to the wife?

Share your answers, then talk about how you are doing during the first few moments when you arrive home. How easy is it to be perfunctory, preoccupied, and self-absorbed with your own needs? Is Emerson saying couples have to spend a lot of time reconnecting? What is more important—quantity or quality? Take a good look at what the two of you have been doing to reconnect after a busy day. What is your typical routine? Is Emerson right when he says, "The first few moments of reconnecting will set the tone for the rest of the evening"? If you agree with him, you may want to talk about changing your usual routine and spending at least a few minutes talking about what each of you did that day—achievements, frustrations, humorous incidents . . .

10 How important is face-to-face connection? (Read "What My Four-Year-Old Taught Me . . ." book pages 127–28.) Question for husbands: How are you doing at face-to-face with your wife? Question for wives: How can you respectfully ask your husband for more face-to-face connecting? (See *Love & Respect* Appendix C, under "Wives can humbly and softly say," page 311.)

 Not every husband will appreciate being confronted about his face-to-face time with his wife, particularly if he hasn't been doing it that much. Wives should be sensitive to this. In addition, Emerson adds an important point: "If a wife wants to encourage her husband to be close face-to-face, she must always consider what her face looks like. I'm not talking about looking like some cover girl; I mean the facial expression, which can be sweet and welcoming or sour and rejecting. From his extensive research with thousands of married couples, John Gottman concluded that 'Wives who make sour facial expressions when their husbands talk are likely to be separated within four years.'[i] When a husband does move toward a wife face-to-face, she should think about showing respectful interest. At the same time the husband should place importance on looking like he wants to be close and loving, not like he is in a board meeting. For both spouses the emphasis is always on being humble and gentle as you seek to meet each other's needs."

11 Read the sections entitled, "Involvement or Independence?" and "Only Chickens Get Henpecked" (book pages 128–30). Then mark the line below according to what you need—more involvement with your spouse or more independence from your spouse.

Involvement ——————————————————— **Independence**

 According to Emerson, "In the typical marriage relationship, she leans more toward the 'Involvement' side while he leans more toward the 'Independence' side." Talk together about the amount of tension you see in your marriage,

i John Gottman, *Why Marriages Succeed or Fail* (New York: Simon & Schuster, 1994), back cover.

between her need for involvement and his need for independence. Remember, this kind of tension is normal, so think positively about how you can solve his need for 'space' and her need to be 'close.' If this subject isn't too sensitive, discuss what Emerson says on book page 129 about a wife not wanting her husband to become like a "girl friend," but how even small moves toward closeness by the husband can energize the wife. Wife, do you agree? Husband, are you willing to give up a little independence in order to be a little closer to your wife? What might happen if you did? For more tips and helps for talking together about something like this, see *Love & Respect* Appendix A, page 305–307, especially "Always ask yourself," "Things to remember," and "Things to say to lighten up the relationship."

12 According to Emerson, there is a battle to the death going on between the Crazy Cycle and the Energizing Cycle (pages 130–31). What suggestions does he make in this section to help husbands win that battle and have a great marriage? Check off phrases that sound helpful to you, or write down your own ideas.

____ Always seek to motivate and not demoralize.

____ Always be trying to adjust your "sunglasses" and "hearing aids."

____ Always try to do the positive, loving thing.

____ I think:

While this question is directed primarily at helping husbands love their wives, the suggestions listed above can easily be used by wives who want to respect their husbands. Do you both agree with Emerson's assertion that "this is a war—a battle to the death between the Crazy Cycle and the Energizing Cycle"? Why or why not?

———

13 Chapter Nine closes with tips and techniques for being close (book pages 131–33). Go down the list and find things that you are doing well. Then find one thing that you have not done for a while. Write it here, then plan how you can do it in the next twenty-four hours.

 Husband, take time to ask your wife what she would like. (Maybe she will just want you to surprise her.)

A JOURNAL OF MY JOURNEY TO LOVE AND RESPECT

Always take at least a few minutes to write down your feelings, questions, insights gained, and other comments when you finish a study session. Months, or even years, from now, you will appreciate reviewing this record of your growth as a person and a spouse.

Scripture Meditations

1. "When I found him whom my soul loves; I held on to him and would not let him go" (Song of Solomon 3:4). A woman in love longs for closeness. Husband, does your wife's need for face-to-face closeness seem like "clinging" to you? At the same time, is it okay for her to request face-to-face talking and physical closeness without wanting sexual intimacy? Serious tension can develop if a husband constantly reads his wife's desire for closeness as an invitation to have sex. What can a couple do if this is the case? One solution that I have seen work in many marriages is getting on a schedule to take the guesswork out of when you will be sexually intimate. This kind of schedule leads in turn to regular, scheduled times for face-to-face interaction without the husband pushing the sexual issue, because he knows the schedule. Does this sound rigid and non-spontaneous? Nonetheless, it can work miracles in a marriage.

2. A wife always hopes, "Now my husband will hold me close" (Genesis 29:34 CEV). Husband, have you ever heard your wife say, "I need a hug"? God seems to have made women for closeness and hugs. When women friends greet each other, do they hug or shake hands? For a group photo, do several women stand shoulder to shoulder as men would do, or do they squeeze close together, almost cheek to cheek for the camera? When your wife wants you to hold her close in a nonsexual way, does she have some problem with you, or is she simply a woman expressing her womanly desires? Is she wrong for having these desires, or just different from you? If you have not been that aware of this female need for hugs and closeness that don't always lead to sex, what little change will you make that can make a huge difference in your wife's feeling loved?

3. As Paul seeks to advise the Corinthians concerning a dispute that had arisen in their church, he says, "In the Lord, however, woman is not independent of man, nor is man independent of woman" (1 Corinthians 11:11 NIV). In other words, the basic New Testament principle is that women and men are equal before God. Eugene Peterson puts it well when he paraphrases this verse in *The Message*: "Neither man nor woman can go it alone or claim priority." there is great truth here for today's Love and Respect couple: there is always the temptation to become too independent of one another, particularly on the man's part. Because a man leaves father and mother (Genesis 2:24),

his tendency is toward independence. The typical man, who does not have the same emotional need to connect as his wife does, should continually ask himself some important questions: Am I choosing activities that keep me too far away from her? Am I engaging in activities that keep me too independent and justifying them as "my right" or "something I need"? Do I sometimes change my plans but do not bother to inform her? Do I take on still more responsibilities (for example, in the church, on the job, in the community) even though my wife is overwhelmed at home with our children? Do I withhold information from her that she should know? Do I make decisions without including her, even though these decisions impact her significantly? Go over these questions, and anything else where your wife may be complaining about your being too independent (not involved enough at home). If the answer to any of these questions is yes, perhaps it is time to talk and pray with her about changes you could make.

My current thoughts about our marriage:

Session Six

In preparation for this session, read Chapter Ten, "Openness—She Wants You to Open Up to Her," and Chapter Eleven, "Understanding—Don't Try to 'Fix' Her; Just Listen." The following questions are for study by an individual or by a husband and wife together. Remember to answer all unmarked questions first, then answer questions marked by the male or female icon (whichever applies to you). Finally, answer the questions with the couple icon, if you're studying with your mate. (Suggestions for anyone planning to use this study with a small group can be found in *Workbook* Appendix I, page 201.)

Questions for Chapter Ten

1 As he begins Chapter Ten (book page 135) Emerson shares from his counseling experience, describing how couples act when they come in to see him. Men tend to be closed, playing it close to the vest. The wife is much more open, wanting to talk and connect with her husband. Does this describe you and your spouse—the husband more quiet and closed, the wife more open and talkative?

FITS US PERFECTLY ____   SOMEWHAT TRUE OF US ____   NOT TRUE OF US AT ALL ____

 Compare your answers. If you both believe this is true of the two of you, at least to some degree, talk about it as much as feels comfortable. The typically "closed" husband may not want to go into it to any extent, at least at this time in your study. (Note that it is also possible for a wife to be closed, which could be perfectly normal for her. And, there are husbands who are quite expressive. If this reverse situation is true of your marriage, discuss how it affects your communication. For more on "exceptions" to the Love and Respect norm, see *Love & Respect* Appendix D, page 313.)

2 Read the material "Smash One of Her Lights . . ." (book pages 136–37) very carefully. It is one of the most important analogies in this entire workbook. Emerson illustrates the difference between the typically expressive-responsive wife and the typically compartmentalized husband by picturing two electrical circuits, both with 3000 lights. On the first circuit, if you smash just one light, the whole thing shuts down. On the second circuit, if you smash two thousand lights, the other thousand will stay lit. According to Emerson's explanation, why is the expressive-responsive wife like the first circuit? Why is the compartmentalized husband like the second?

Compare notes on what you wrote down concerning the electric circuits analogy. It will probably be useful to read pages 136–37 together to grasp how important it is that the husband understands how one minor tiff can affect his wife all day and still be bothering her when they reconnect at day's end. The husband has probably forgotten all about whatever happened earlier because he has compartmentalized it—shoved it aside where it can't bother him. His wife, however, is an integrated personality who does not compartmentalize things. Everything is connected and one small remark that hurts her stays with her until the hurt is repaired. Talk together about what this can mean to each of you in different situations, for example, if you are invited out for the evening . . . if you planned to work together on something related to the house . . . if he hoped to make love that evening.

3 In "Wives See Husbands As Mysterious Islands" (book pages 137–39), Emerson describes a typical phenomenon: the husband is open, communicative, and charming during courtship, but after getting married he closes up. Why does this happen? How does it make the marriage vulnerable to the Crazy Cycle?

This could be a sensitive question, particularly if the husband thinks he is being accused of doing one thing during courtship and then the reverse after marriage. Compare what you wrote and talk about what is comfortable for both of you. His "closing down" after marriage could well be his not fully understanding how to love his wife properly. He is good-willed, but unaware (and possibly quite willing to learn). On the other hand, it is quite possible that after they got married, his wife started criticizing and being disrespectful, and then he closed up. Do not dwell on deciding if it was "the chicken or the egg." Talk together about adjustments you both can make right now to keep the Crazy Cycle from starting to spin. And always be aware of the possibility that, basically, you may already be married to a loving husband or a respectful wife. There are things you can improve upon, but 80 percent or more of your marriage already consists of love and respect. If this is the case, be thankful and build on that foundation.

4 Do you keep your wife up-to-date? Read "Sarah Prefers . . ." (book pages 139–40) and see if you have ever struggled (or perhaps you are struggling now) as Emerson did. Following are questions a husband could ask himself if he is tempted to think his wife is snooping or prying. How he answers each question can tell him a great deal concerning why he may not be keeping his wife informed. (**Wives should answer these questions as well.**)

Is my wife a good-willed woman?	YES ___	NO ___
Is she trying to control me?	YES ___	NO ___
Is she trying to connect and be close?	YES ___	NO ___
Is she trying to make me feel guilty?	YES ___	NO ___

Share with each other how you answered the questions above from your individual perspectives. If the husband perceives the wife as coming across as "prying or controlling," this is her chance to reassure him of her good intentions. And if the husband realizes he has been reading his wife wrong (decoding her incorrectly), this is his chance to apologize for misinterpreting her heart, to say that he is sorry and from now on he will try to do a better job of decoding (and keeping her up-to-date).

5 In "Beware of Becoming Embittered" (book pages 140–42), Emerson describes a disturbing problem that can be caused when a husband is closed toward his wife. As he withdraws and refuses to talk about much of anything, the husband can appear to be irritated, even bitter. His wife thinks he is secretly (or not so secretly) angry with her. What can a husband do to guard against coming across as bitter or harsh? See Colossians 3:19, and especially the letters from wives on page 142, for some simple but powerful ideas. Write down some things that may be useful in your marriage.

This question may be a sensitive one for discussion. If a husband is embittered because he secretly feels his wife is disrespectful, he may want to justify his attitude instead of seeing his wife's need for love. And if the wife is hurt by his harshness or irritation she will want to judge him as unloving and minimize her own disrespectful actions. Good-willed spouses who don't want to hang on to being angry or hurt over past problems can work their way into a discussion by comparing what they found in the letters from wives on book page 142. Also, if both of you are comfortable with the idea, look at Colossians 3:19 together. Paul's words are God's command to the husband to love his wife and not be embittered toward her. Why is bitterness never effective, always destructive? If a husband tries to use bitterness to "teach his wife a lesson," what kind of "lesson" will she learn? (Also note: As a husband, you may be saying this question is not for you, because you're not bitter.

Nonetheless, husbands must always guard against sounding or looking bitter with a harsh tone or dark countenance. If a wife is perceiving her husband as "bitter and angry," which of the following are the most useful: a loving look, a friendly gesture, a gentler tone? All of these?)

———

6 To close Chapter Ten, Emerson asks husbands a practical question: "How Will You Then Live with This Sensitive Creature?" (book pages 143–44). As a husband, what practical ideas do you find on these pages that you can or should use? As a wife, what do you see on these pages that you would like to respectfully point out to your husband?

Compare what you found on pages 143–44. Husband, did you ask yourself, "How often do I come off as harsh when I'm just telling her what I think?" Wife, did you think about, "How sensitive am I to my husband's words and moods? Am I letting him know tactfully and respectfully when he steps on my air hose because he sounds harsh?"

———

7 On book page 144, just before the chapter on openness ends, is some excellent advice for husbands concerning sex. According to Emerson, which of the following statements is true?

    ___ To get sex I must try to appear to be more open.

    ___ If I am genuinely open to my wife, she is more likely to be open with me sexually.

 Talk together about the right answer, which is rather obvious, but not necessarily easy to practice for the typical husband. While the husband must be sensitive to his wife's need for openness, she needs to be sensitive to his need for sex. This will be covered more thoroughly in Session 12.

———

8 Look over the list of tips on book page 144. Husband, which ones are you already using? Which ones are you going to try? Wife, which of these tips would you like to have your husband try?

 Share together about these ideas and how they might help your relationship. For starters, a husband should try at least one idea that he and his wife agree would be helpful.

Questions for Chapter Eleven

9 Chapter Eleven opens with a discussion of 1 Peter 3:7, which says a husband should live with his wife in an understanding way because she is the "weaker partner" (NIV) or "weaker vessel" (NKJV). Feminists tend to bristle at this, claiming it says men are stronger, and therefore superior to women. What has been your understanding of

"weaker partner"? Write your thoughts here, then compare them to Emerson's explanation of what the verse means on book pages 145–46.

 Discuss what you each wrote about 1 Peter 3:7. What do you think Emerson means when he says the wife is the weaker vessel (or partner) "because of her vulnerability to her husband within the marriage relationship"?

10 In "Always Handle Porcelain with Care" (book pages 146–47), wives are seen as porcelain bowls and husbands as copper bowls. Is this a good analogy? Why or why not? What does this comparison have to do with the husband needing to "understand" his wife?

Compare notes on your reaction to the porcelain/copper analogy. Talk about times when a wife wants to be "handled with care." What are some specific ways a husband can do this?

⌒

11 The bottom half of page 147 talks about something you may have noticed: The principles in C-O-U-P-L-E connect and even overlap. How can practicing closeness and openness help a husband with understanding his wife? Write your ideas here.

 Compare what you wrote. As you work on the rest of this session, take note when anything you wrote above matches up with some of the key truths in the rest of Chapter Eleven.

⌒

12 Read book pages 148–51. What does Sarah usually want from Emerson—a "solution" or a listening ear? How is the man's typical desire to "fix" whatever seems to be wrong an example of "blue" thinking? How is the woman's typical desire to "just want to talk" an example of "pink" thinking?

Compare yourselves with Sarah and Emerson. Does the wife usually want to "just talk"? Does the husband prefer to exchange information, come to conclusions, or "fix a problem"? If the two of you fit this profile, how does it sometimes lead to problems? What can each of you do about it?

———

13 "'Just Talking' Is a Key . . ." (book pages 151–52) presents some valuable help for men who are trying to show their wives understanding. Husbands, read this section carefully, then list key phrases and sentences you want to remember and ideas you want to try. Wives, what do you see in this section that describes you? How important is "just talking" to you?

 Compare notes on what you have each written above. If "just talking" is even moderately important to the wife, she can elaborate on why this is true. Wise husbands will "just listen" and try to understand.

14 Do you agree that "Understanding Takes Scheduled Time"? (See book pages 152–54.) How does this idea strike you? Be totally honest.

_____ a. I agree completely and already do this, or plan to do this regularly.

_____ b. I'm not sure it would work . . . What would we talk about?

_____ c. I'd like to try it, but doubt we have the time.

_____ d. I think understanding is something you feel, not something you schedule.

_____ e. I think:

 Compare answers, then discuss how useful it would be to schedule time to talk. (See Emerson's additional comments on answers *b*, *c*, and *d* in *Workbook* Appendix VI.)

15 Look over the list of tips at the bottom of book page 154. Husbands, pick at least one thing you will try this coming week. Wives, choose at least one thing you would like your husband to try this coming week. Write your choices here.

 Compare your choices and agree on what the husband is going to try. (The wife should not be judgmental if her husband doesn't perform flawlessly. Be encouraging as he tries things that are probably new to him.)

A Journal of My Journey to Love and Respect

Take time to add your thoughts to the points below as you continue to create a record of your journey toward Love and Respect.

Scripture Meditations

1. Proverbs 31:12 says, "She does him good and not evil all the days of her life." Do you believe this about your wife? Does this motivate you to be more open with her?

2. The wise husband is "quick to listen, slow to speak" (James 1:19 NIV). As you deal with your wife, do you find it easier to give solutions or give empathy (put yourself in her shoes and think about how she feels)? If you are more solution-oriented, recall a recent conversation with your wife where it would have been better to listen than to speak. Would it help to pray daily asking God to help you be more empathy-oriented?

3. In 1 Peter 3:7, the apostle tells husbands to ". . . live with your wives in an understanding way . . . show her honor as a fellow heir of the grace of life." God has made your wife with needs and vulnerabilities that are different from yours. Can you name some of them? Do you find yourself being impatient with some of her needs or vulnerabilities? How can you begin treating her with more understanding and respect in one or two of these areas?

My current thoughts about our marriage:

SESSION SEVEN

In preparation for this session, read Chapter Twelve, "Peacemaking—She Wants You to Say, 'I'm Sorry.'" The following questions are for study by an individual or by a husband and wife studying together. Remember to answer all unmarked questions first, then answer questions marked by the male or female icon (whichever applies to you). Finally, answer the questions with the couple icon, if you're studying with your mate. (Suggestions for anyone planning to use this study with a small group can be found in *Workbook* Appendix I, page 201.)

1 On book page 156, Emerson introduces what he calls "the fourth side to connectivity"—peacemaking—and adds that it might be even more important than the three principles you have studied so far in C-O-U-P-L-E: closeness, openness, and understanding. As you began reading this chapter, what was your response to seeing peacemaking as a major principle for a husband to employ in "spelling love to his wife"? Choose from the statements below, or write your own response.

_____ a. "Peacemaking" suggests there has been a fight; frankly, I always try to avoid conflict. I just want us to get on with our lives.

_____ b. The best way to resolve a fight is to speak your mind and then drop it and move on.

_____ c. I don't want to sound arrogant, but if my spouse would defer to my good judgments we wouldn't have these arguments and peace would reign.

_____ d. Feeling at peace, because things are up-to-date with nothing between us, has a lot to do with my feeling okay about our relationship.

_____ e. I think:

Husband, which of the comments above captures your feelings? Wife, which statement captures yours? As this session of study will show, it is vital for a wife to feel at peace, with nothing between her and her husband.

2 Continuing on book page 156, Emerson mentions a "paradox" he found as he studied the Scriptures: "God intended for some conflict to exist in a marriage." He goes on to say that secular research confirms that the best marriage relationships have conflict and that it almost seems that a marriage needs to have some conflict to keep the passion in it. What do you think? Do you agree that conflict puts just enough spice in marriage? Choose from these responses, or write your own:

___ a. Sometimes conflict helps; sometimes it doesn't.

___ b. Conflict is never good; it squelches passion for me.

___ c. A little conflict is good, because it's fun to make up afterward.

___ d. I think:

 Discuss your answers, then compare your conclusions to what Emerson says about the risk involved when "the sparks fly" (book pages 156–57).

3 In "Husband and Wife Can 'Work It Out,'" book pages 157–58, Emerson makes some comments that may be new to you concerning how spouses can deal with conflict in their marriage. Read these pages carefully, then jot down phrases or sentences that strike you as a different approach to working out conflict. (If you are study-

ing with your spouse, you can discuss what you find at this point, or wait until Question 4.)

---

4 What in particular does Emerson say on book pages 157–58 about how couples should view a conflict over sex? To put it in practical terms: "Tonight, after a particularly stressful day for both of you, who decides if you will be sexually intimate? First Corinthians 7:3–5 says both spouses have authority over the other's body, so who decides?" When Emerson speaks at Love and Respect Conferences, his answer to this question is: "Yes!" This usually gets a laugh, but the real answer is found in 1 Corinthians 7:5, plus what Emerson says on page 158. How would you sum up his description on page 158 of "one of the great principles of the New Testament"?

 Discuss the ideas you both put down, then compare your conclusions with Emerson's further thoughts on this crucial question. (See Emerson's additional comments in *Workbook* Appendix VI.)

---

5 In "My Wife Is Always Getting Historical," book pages 158–60, Emerson gives husbands another important tip for making peace. Husband, as you read this section, think about how "historical" your wife has been or can be. Does she bewilder you with her seemingly endless memory? Wives, how do you see yourself regarding your tendency to "get historical" with your husband?

    ___ a. Extremely historical (memory like an elephant)

    ___ b. Somewhat historical (might bring something up now and then)

    ___ c. Not historical at all (never bring up anything from the past)

    ___ d. I think:

 Compare your perceptions. What does the husband think of his wife's historical propensities? Does she agree that she can be historical? Discuss your answers. If tension begins to rise, try to keep things light: "May I borrow your pink/blue hearing aids? I need help understanding what you're trying to say." (For more "lighten things up" ideas see *Love & Respect* Appendix A, page 307.)

6 According to book page 160, why is it usually not helpful for the husband to say, "Let's drop it—just forget it"? At the bottom of page 160, what does Emerson recommend a husband say if he wants to make peace with his wife? Write out these three short sentences below and commit them to memory.

Take plenty of time to discuss this one. Be sure to read the letter from the frustrated wife on book page 160. Work together on the real issue: love for her, respect for him.

———

7 The section captioned "Why It's Hard for a Man to Say, 'I'm Sorry'" (book pages 161–62) offers important insights on how men think. Emerson speaks from experience when he observes: "When a woman says, 'I'm sorry,' to her it's an increase of love. But when a man says, 'I'm sorry,' he fears he will lose respect." Do you agree or disagree with his observation? What does your experience tell you?

____ a. I agree on all counts.

____ b. I partially agree.

____ c. I disagree on all counts.

____ d. I think (write your reasons for your answer above):

———

8 Read the story about the couple who had a childish fight, but then he said the words that made her "fall in love with him all over again." Why is saying, "I'm sorry" so powerful? What dynamics are at work?

Discuss your answers and share what you think of Emerson's belief that when a husband humbly expresses sorrow for what he did, his wife melts. He doesn't think many men "grasp" this. Is he right?

9 Which points made in "A Short Course on Peacemaking," book pages 162–64, are most helpful, in your opinion? Some of the more obvious ideas are listed below. Choose from these, or find others you like as much or better:

_____ a. A husband should have absolute confidence in the power of his loving demeanor (see Proverbs 15:1).

_____ b. When a husband says he is sorry, he must be sure he means it, or be ready for another spin on the Crazy Cycle.

_____ c. The husband will make peace with his wife when he doesn't blame her but, instead, confesses his part of the blame (see James 5:16).

_____ d. When a husband says, "I'm sorry," it's a big turn on for a woman, but an even bigger turn-on is when he adds, "I think I understand your feelings and why you react as you do. Will you forgive me?"

_____ e. If a husband utters sincere words of apology, forgiveness, and love, his wife will trust his words and trust him. It can heal the whole thing.

_____ f. Other points I like:

The wife should be sure to fill out her answers to the above question along with her husband. Discussing your ideas can give you both more insights into how each of you thinks.

10. Chapter Twelve closes with a list of tips: "She'll Feel at Peace with You When . . ." (book page 164). Do you see anything else here that would help the peace-making process in your marriage?

As you compare notes on this question, you might want to review your answers to Question 9. Then, agree on one thing the husband can do differently during the coming week. When he attempts to practice what you both have agreed upon, if at all possible, stop and talk about how it worked, how it felt. Always be positive and encouraging to one another. If he makes real progress on his "one thing to do differently" go over the tips and ideas again and choose another action or attitude he can use to improve your peacemaking process.

A JOURNAL OF MY JOURNEY TO LOVE AND RESPECT

Build another "chapter" of your journal to Love and Respect by interacting with the following points.

SCRIPTURE MEDITATIONS

1. After giving advice to wives and husbands in 1 Peter 3:1–7, Peter writes this summary: ". . . all of you be harmonious, sympathetic, brotherly, kindhearted, and humble in spirit" (v. 8). As a spouse, which of these do you do best? Which does your spouse do best? Do you both bring strengths to the marriage that can make for peace?

2. "If possible, so far as it depends on you, be at peace with all men" (Romans 12:18). Peace is possible if you believe the other person wants to be at peace with you and will

respond if you take the initiative. As a husband, do you have faith that if you were to apologize for being unloving, your wife would respond? As a wife, do you have faith that if you were to apologize for being disrespectful, your husband would respond? If your answer is yes, then as far as it depends on you, you can be at peace with your spouse.

3. "Be humble in the presence of God's mighty power, and he will honor you when the time comes" (1 Peter 5:6 CEV). We fear that if we seek to make peace by humbling ourselves and confessing our lack of love and respect, our spouse will not reciprocate. Ultimately, however, this is not about our humility before our spouse, but being humble in the presence of God. According to this verse, when we are humble in the presence of God what eventually happens? How can we have the courage to humble ourselves in this way (see v. 7)?

My current thoughts about our marriage:

SESSION EIGHT

In preparation for this session, read Chapter Thirteen, "Loyalty—She Needs to Know You're Committed," and Chapter Fourteen, "Esteem—She Wants You to Honor and Cherish Her." The following questions are for an individual or a husband and wife studying together. Remember to answer all unmarked questions first, then answer questions marked by the male or female icon (whichever applies to you). Finally, answer the questions with the couple icon, if you're studying with your mate. (Suggestions for anyone planning to use this workbook with a small group can be found in *Workbook* Appendix I, page 201.)

Questions for Chapter Thirteen

1 Read the opening of Chapter Thirteen on book page 165. What are your first impressions of the idea that a wife needs reassurance of her husband's love?

 Which of the following responses comes close to yours? (Or write your own.)

____ a. I'm well aware that my wife needs reassurance of my love, and I try to provide it whenever I see (or hear) that she needs it.

____ b. Have never thought much about it—she knows I love her, why do I have to keep telling her?

____ c. Reassurance? Every time I try to tell her I love her, she tells me I don't mean it, or I'm just saying that because I want sex.

____ d. I think:

What is your reaction to page 165? Is reassurance of your husband's love something you like to hear fairly often? Check the answer that comes close to your ideas (or write your own).

____ a. Reassurance is important to me, and I think most women feel the same.

____ b. I've had my husband use that "Don't worry, I'm not going to trade you in for a new model" line, and I didn't think it was that funny.

____ c. My husband is always telling me he loves me, and I never get tired of hearing it.

____ d. I think:

Compare notes on your answers checked or written above. If you both feel about the same concerning the importance of a husband's loyalty, be encouraged. On the other hand, it is possible the two of you will not agree on the importance of loyalty, or even what loyalty looks like in a marriage. For example, it is not unusual for the husband to be rather unaware of how important it is to reassure his wife of his loyalty and his love. The good-willed husband who falls into this category should be willing to learn as he proceeds with this session.

───────

2 Read the letter from the wife at the top of book page 166. How does her husband reassure her? Are there any key words or principles you appreciate or find useful? Write them here:

Compare notes on what you see in the wife's letter that might be helpful in your own marriage. Spend some time on how the wife tells her husband she feels "emotionally disconnected" from him at certain times and what he does about it. Is "I'm feeling disconnected" something one or both of you might be able to say to communicate a need, or would it just trigger arguments?

───────

3 Read the sections "She's a One-Man Woman . . ." and "It's a 'Swimsuit Issue' World," book pages 166–68. Is a wife being overly sensitive if she wonders about her husband's commitment, particularly with the barrage of beautiful females that bombard his eyes daily—in person and in the media? Choose from the following answers, or write your own opinion.

____ a. A wife can't help but wonder sometimes.

____ b. Either spouse might struggle with commitment.

____ c. It would be nice for a wife to be reassured now and then, especially as her body reflects the aging process.

_____ d. What's a man to do? His wife should know he might look, but she has nothing to worry about.

_____ e. I think:

 This can be a sensitive issue, so beware of stepping on your mate's air hose. Try comparing the answers you checked or wrote. Wife, if you do feel at least a little insecure, let your husband know without condemning him. Husband, how can you reassure your wife of your commitment? Does Job have some good advice when he says: "I made a covenant with my eyes not to look lustfully at a girl" (Job 31:1 NIV)?

4 How does Song of Solomon 8:6 catch a wife's deep feelings about needing to always be sure of her husband's loyalty? Also read Emerson's thoughts on the wedding ring (book page 168). Why is a wedding ring so important? Write your ideas here:

 Be sure not to skip this one. Share honestly with each other about your perspective on wearing a wedding ring. Is Emerson right when he says: "No husband should leave home without one"? Why or why not?

5 The prophet Malachi warned Israel against the prevalent practice of easy divorce that was going on in Israel as husbands dealt treacherously with their wives (see Malachi 2:14–15). Read "Are You Being As Loyal As You Could Be?" (book pages 168–69). Emerson is not saying that today's good-willed husband is trying to be treacherous toward his wife—but what is he saying? How can heeding Malachi 2:14–15 help keep you and your spouse off the Crazy Cycle?

Discuss your answers to this question with sensitivity to each other. Try to dwell on the positive idea that "his love motivates her respect." A big part of a husband's love for his wife is being loyal in every way he can think of. In Malachi 2:16, the prophet tells husbands, ". . . take heed to your spirit, that you do not deal treacherously [with your wives]." Is this passage only for husbands in Malachi's time, or is this also a warning for today's husband to be on guard against things that can undermine faithfulness to God and his wife? What are some of those "things" that can tempt a husband to be unfaithful?

6 On book pages 169–70 read the story of Robertson McQuilken, who left his position as a seminary president to care for his wife who was slowly dying of Alzheimer's disease. What does McQuilken's "sacrifice" tell you about the meaning of being loyal as a husband? Write down some of the thoughts he expressed when he faced his decision.

You and your mate may want to read Robertson McQuilken's story together, then share your thoughts. See especially the quote, "Almost all women stand by their men; very few men stand by their women." How can a good-willed husband turn this statement from a possible guilt trip into a motivator to be more loyal to his wife?

7 Which of the tips included in "She Is Assured of Your Loyalty When . . ." (book pages 171–72) could be a real help in sparking the Energizing Cycle for your marriage? Pick out one and write a brief reason why this particular idea could help you and your spouse.

Compare your choices, then agree on which tip the husband should practice during the coming week. If you each have a strong preference, perhaps he can practice both ideas. Be sure to talk about and encourage what he decides to live out on a daily basis.

Questions for Chapter Fourteen

8 Wives often ask where Scripture talks about the husband respecting his wife. On book pages 173–75 Emerson spells out what it means for a husband to respect (honor and cherish) his wife. (See especially 1 Peter 3:7.) Which of the following ideas, taken from this section, are most useful to you as a spouse?

_____ a. God has made women so that they want to be esteemed, honored, and respected.

_____ b. The honor a wife seeks is a different kind of honor from what her husband seeks as a man.

_____ c. To your wife, respect, honor, and esteem are not qualities in and of themselves; they are components of the love she wants from you.

_____ d. Other:

 A wife studying with her husband should be sure to give her opinion on this one to see how closely it matches her husband's choices. Talk together about Emerson's claim, "Your wife wants to know that you have her on your mind and heart first and foremost. This is what I mean by 'esteem'; when it's there, your wife will feel treasured as if she's the most loved woman on earth" (book page 175). Do you both agree he is right?

9 In "Our Kids Often Made Sarah Feel . . ." (book pages 175–76) Emerson shares a practical way he esteemed his wife, Sarah, at a critical time in their marriage. What did he do, and why was it effective?

If you have children growing up in your home, this story can be very applicable to your marriage at this time. Parenting is difficult at best. What does the final paragraph in the section tell you about why moms usually need more support and encouragement than dads as they do parenting tasks?

10 Back in Session 1, question 8 dealt with the time Emerson forgot Sarah's birthday—completely! This was good for several more turns on the Crazy Cycle for both of them. For further insight on how much store women put in birthdays and anniversaries, read "Use Symbols to Show Your Wife Esteem" (book pages 176–79). Following are some quotes from this section. Write down your response to each of Emerson's observations, whether you agree or disagree and why.

a. "You will never be able to show her the amount of emotional openness and esteem that she really wants—no man could—but symbolic things can do a great deal to bridge the gap."

AGREE ____   DISAGREE ____   **Explain:**

b. "Women are the ones who have babies, and that's one reason that birthdays are a big deal to them. . . . In a woman's mind, who could possibly forget a birthday? She never would."

AGREE ____   DISAGREE ____   **Explain:**

c. ". . . a marriage date is etched in the woman's soul. Since childhood, your wife dreamed of the wedding day. . . ."

AGREE ____   DISAGREE ____   **Explain:**

 This section offers some great discussion possibilities. As a wife, do you feel about birthdays and anniversaries the way Emerson describes? As a husband, do you begin to grasp how important this can be to a woman?

Discuss the example of giving the wife a Mercedes or a little rock with a sentimental message inscribed on it (see book page 178). Is Emerson overstating his case when he claims most women would treasure the rock more? What is his point? And be sure to read the letter from the wife whose husband "went all out" for Valentine's Day. Should more husbands try things like this? Why or why not?

---

11 Read the story included in "Does Your Wife Ever Want . . ." (book pages 179–81). Is Emerson right when he says, "Every husband has been expected to read his wife's mind"? What do you think of Emerson's suggested solution to the husband's problem when his wife doesn't want to go to the restaurant he picked? Is coming up with some alternative restaurants too much to ask of the typical husband?

The two of you can have fun with this story, as long as it doesn't crimp somebody's air hose. (You may want to borrow each other's pink or blue sunglasses and hearing aids!) For other ways to lighten up the discussion see book page 307. Also talk about how a husband can disagree with his wife and keep her esteem intact (see the last paragraph in the section, page 181, where Emerson offers three responses a husband can make). What is the key to disagreeing agreeably?

12. Read "Thank Her for All She Does" and "Your Wife Will Feel Esteemed When . . ." (book pages 181–82). Which of these ideas and tips for ways to make a wife feel esteemed seem most practical to you? Write down your choices and when you plan to try them.

 Be sure the wife gets to contribute her opinion on what the husband might like to try. Later, after the husband tries at least one of these tips, talk about the difference it made and how this practice can be continued.

A Journal of My Journey to Love and Respect

When you have opportunity, review the journal entries you have made since beginning your journey to Love and Respect. Are you encouraged by your progress?

SCRIPTURE MEDITATIONS

1. Because Christians live in a secular culture, they are susceptible to the argument that it is unrealistic for two people to remain faithful to each other "'til death us do part." More than one Christian husband or wife has rationalized, "A person's needs change. In fact we just aren't the same people we were when we got married. I need to move on. I know God wants me to be happy." Is there any passage in the Bible that can "divorce-proof" your marriage? We know God "hates divorce" and He advises all husbands, "So guard yourself in your spirit, and do not break faith with the wife of your youth" Malachi 2:15 NIV). But on the positive side, what can a husband do? Proverbs 5:18–19 offers wisdom: ". . . may you rejoice in the wife of your youth. A loving doe, a graceful deer—may her breasts satisfy you always, may you ever be captivated by her love" (NIV). Not only does this passage assume that a marriage is to be long and lasting, but it tells us how to make it so. The loyal husband not only refuses to gaze on other women, but he fixes his eyes on his wife, refusing to see the negative, and rejoicing in her positive features and the loving person she is.

2. A woman never tires of hearing her husband call her "my darling, my beautiful one" (Song of Solomon 2:10). In your opinion, why is this true? Have you, husband, said this to your wife lately?

3. "Does a young woman forget all about her jewelry? Does a bride forget her wedding jewels?" (Jeremiah 2:32 NIRV). What is the prophet saying about the nature of the female? Is there any such language about men in the Bible? Why did God design women to remember in detail and forever those things related to being the object of her husband's loyal love? Her wedding jewels (today, her wedding ring) symbolize her husband's loyal love, reserved only for her. Do you as a husband appreciate how God designed your wife? If you have daughters, are you mindful that He made them the same way? Is it any wonder, then, that if your loyalty wobbles—or appears to wobble—that she will be filled with fear? Is it time to take her out to dinner (or just take her by the hand) and tell her how much you love her, how glad you are God gave her to you?

4. In 1 Peter 3:7 the apostle instructs the husband to live with his wife in an understanding way and to "show her honor as a fellow heir of the grace of life, so that your prayers will not be hindered." Peter continues in the passage (see 1 Peter 3:8–12) with general instructions to all believers on how to live the Christian life and sums up his

teaching with a quote from Psalm 34:15–16: "For the eyes of the Lord are upon the righteous, and his ears attend to their prayer, but the face of the Lord is against those who do evil." The entire passage (vs. 7–12) shows that God watches a good-willed husband who treats his wife with understanding, and that husband's prayers are not hindered. One husband wrote Emerson to say, "You spoke of our prayers being hindered due to our relationships with our wives. Well, it hit me like a ton of bricks. I knew something was hindering my prayers, but this opened a new door to me." Questions for every husband: "Am I honoring my wife, esteeming her for all she is and does? Or are my prayers being hindered in any way because of how I treat her?"

My current thoughts about our marriage:

SESSION NINE

In preparation for this session, read Chapter Fifteen, "C-H-A-I-R-S: How to Spell Respect to Your Husband," and Chapter Sixteen, "Conquest—Appreciate His Desire to Work and Achieve." The following questions are for individual study or study by a couple. Remember to answer all unmarked questions first, then answer questions marked by the male or female icon (whichever applies to you). Finally, answer the questions with the couple icon, if you're studying with your mate. (Suggestions for leading a small group in studying this workbook can be found in *Workbook* Appendix I, page 201.)

This session opens your study of C-H-A-I-R-S, six principles to help a wife learn important aspects of respecting her husband. Note that just under the title of Chapter Fifteen in *Love & Respect* is a notice to husbands saying the next several chapters are "for wives only but husbands are invited to read along." Husbands are also invited to study along as well, so please do. As the wife discusses the six parts of C-H-A-I-R-S with the husband, she will learn more about how to respect him (and he will learn how to help and encourage her to do it better!).

A SPECIAL WORD FOR WIVES FROM EMERSON:

What I told the husbands about how to use C-O-U-P-L-E (book page 118) also applies to wives regarding their acronym, C-H-A-I-R-S. The Crazy Cycle says that when a husband is acting unlovingly, there is a good chance he is feeling disrespected. And, as C-H-A-I-R-S explains, there can be six good reasons for this. For example, if he feels you aren't really appreciating his desire to protect and provide for you (hierarchy), he can react in an unloving fashion. As C-O-U-P-L-E serves the husband as a diagnostic tool to figure out what is happening in the marriage, C-H-A-I-R-S plays the same role for the wife. She can say to herself, "Since my husband is acting in ways that feel unloving to me, perhaps it is because he feels disrespected. I can react in one of two ways: be even more disrespectful because he is so unloving, or I can decode by checking C-H-A-I-R-S to see where I might be saying or doing something wrong."

With this approach, you can temper your hurt feelings and resist the temptation to go after him with angry tears or criticism. You can try to decode his words or actions as you trust he is a good-willed man who wishes you no evil (even if it seems that way at the moment). Vital to your decoding process is to remember that C-H-A-I-R-S spells out six desires that are deep in a man's soul, given to him by God. For example, he has a desire to protect and provide, to serve and to lead, and others. Unconditional respect by the wife means she respects these God-given desires, even if her husband doesn't always fulfill them as well as he (or she) would like. (For more on understanding and respecting your husband's God-given desires, visit the Web site: http://loveandrespect.com/pearl/)

In a real sense, C-H-A-I-R-S is your "decoder" as you try to pinpoint what it is you may have done that felt disrespectful to your husband. For example, you recall a recent conversation in the car, when he started to offer his opinion on what should be done to get the kids to do their homework. You remember cutting him off in mid-sentence, saying you had already talked to their teachers and had it all worked out. Obviously, you stepped on his air hose big time in the area of Insight—his desire to analyze and counsel. What can you do? Apologize and ask for forgiveness for being disrespectful. (It also won't hurt if you start asking his opinion about things you have been handling alone because "it's just easier that way.") Chances are he may shrug it off and say "No problem," but deep down he will like being shown respect, if only through an apology. And the Energizing Cycle will start humming again.

As I mentioned to the husbands, there may be times when you can't decode what's wrong. Your best bet is to communicate your feelings with the "need communicator" statements at the bottom of page 306 in *Love & Respect*. Let him know that what he's been doing feels unloving and you wonder if you have done something disrespectful. He may or may not spell something out, but you can go ahead and say, "I'm sorry if I have been disrespectful. Please tell me how I can come across more respectfully." At this point, he may give you some idea of what is bothering him. Remember, many men have a hard time expressing that they feel disrespected and can struggle with describing their feelings. The better you know and understand C-H-A-I-R-S, the more successful you will be in decoding the situation.

Questions for Chapter Fifteen

1 To get started, the six words represented by the acronym C-H-A-I-R-S are listed below. Next to each word is a brief definition. Under each word write what it suggests to you. Does your definition match the one given?

Conquest: His desire to work and achieve.

My definition:

Hierarchy: His desire to protect and provide.

My definition:

Authority: His desire to serve and to lead.

My definition:

Insight: His desire to analyze and counsel.

My definition:

Relationship: His desire for shoulder-to-shoulder friendship.

My definition:

Sexuality: His desire for sexual intimacy.

My definition:

Which of these words piqued your curiosity as a husband or as a wife? Which seems most important to a happy marriage? Why? When the study of C-H-A-I-R-S is complete, come back to this question and see if your opinions have changed and talk about why they may have changed.

2 On the opening pages of Chapter Fifteen, Emerson reviews something he said earlier: for many wives the words "unconditional respect" seem like a foreign term, even an oxymoron. According to Emerson's research and experience with thousands of couples, a wife may buy into the idea of giving her husband unconditional respect, but have trouble with how to go about it. Take a moment to put down your honest thoughts about "unconditional respect" from your pink or blue perspective:

I think "unconditional respect" is:

I think "unconditional respect" is:

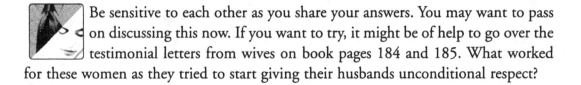 Be sensitive to each other as you share your answers. You may want to pass on discussing this now. If you want to try, it might be of help to go over the testimonial letters from wives on book pages 184 and 185. What worked for these women as they tried to start giving their husbands unconditional respect?

3 "How to Use the 'Respect Test' with Your Husband" (book pages 185–87) includes Emerson's description of one of the most effective tools he has developed to help wives tell their husbands, "I respect you!" Read this section carefully, then record your honest response. Could the Respect Test work in your marriage? Are you willing to try it?

Because you are studying together, obviously it will be impossible for a wife to "surprise" her husband by telling him, "I just want you to know I respect you." Suggestion for wives: write him a "respect note" sometime in the next few days. It doesn't matter if he knows the note is coming. What it says, surprise or not, is what will count. Suggestion for husbands: it is important that you receive and read this note without sarcasm or even teasing such as, "You just wrote this because Emerson told you to." All a husband need remember is how he would feel if he tried to do something loving that is suggested in *Love & Respect*, and his wife responded with, "You're just doing that because you read it in the book." Obviously the whole idea behind saying or writing a message of respect is that the wife wants to do it, even if she isn't sure what will happen.

4 Read the rest of the chapter, from "Be Ready with Reasons That You Respect Him" to the end (book pages 187–92). Emerson stresses that when a wife tells her husband, "I respect you," she must be ready with good reasons why, because he will want to know! A key problem for many wives, especially those just getting acquainted with the concept of respect, is that they can't think of what to say. Look over Emerson's suggestions and make some notes on what could work.

You may agree to leave this question strictly for the wife. If the Respect Test or writing a Respect Note has any favorable results at all (and it usually does) husband and wife will have lots to discuss afterward. As Emerson says on book page 189, the typical good-willed husband wants a happy marriage, and ". . . wives who try the Respect Test can be amazed at what will happen. Men are starving for respect." For examples of what can happen when wives start practicing respect, see the letters on pages 189–91.

Questions for Chapter Sixteen

5 Read the opening of Chapter Sixteen on book pages 193–94, especially the part about what not to say to a man who has lost his job. Why would it probably be nonproductive, even harmful, for a wife to say, "It's okay, honey; we have each other"? What does a man's job have to do with his sense of self-respect? Because his job is so important to him, does that mean his wife is unimportant? Write your thoughts:

Talk together about how important work is to a man. Keep in mind that in this day and age work may be quite important to a woman as well. Later in Chapter Sixteen, Emerson observes that many wives work, but the typical woman likes to have the option of being able to leave the workplace if she so chooses (see book page 199).

6 In "From the Start, Adam Enjoyed His Work" (book pages 194–96), Emerson shares insights from Genesis about the first man and his career path. What does this section tell you about men and their work? Emerson claims that working—being involved in adventure and conquest out in the field of life—is not an option for a man but rather, "it is a deep-seated trait." Write down some of your thoughts about why you agree or disagree with this idea.

Share your reactions to Emerson's opinions. Be sure to discuss what Scripture says about the woman being a "helpmeet" to the man. How does this play out in today's world where many women work out of necessity or choice, and sometimes earn more than their husbands?

7 Read "A Man's First Question: 'What Do You Do?'" (book pages 196–98). What was the real threat to Emerson's two friends who faced dying of cancer?

 The wife should be sure to answer this question and then talk with her husband about his work and its importance. According to the bottom of book page 197, what happens to a husband's air hose if she even implies unknowingly that his work is not all that important?

8 In "Do Women Want to Have It All?" (book pages 198–200), Emerson makes it clear that while women may desire to work out of the home, and may be extremely capable in their jobs, there are questions to ask about how this affects the family, especially the children. Do you agree or disagree with the following statements? Write brief reasons for your answers.

A woman should be able to work if she wants to.

AGREE _____   DISAGREE _____

If at all possible, the man should be the main breadwinner.

AGREE _____   DISAGREE _____

A woman should be able to stop working if she wishes (to take care of a new baby, for example).

AGREE _____   DISAGREE _____

Although there can be exceptions, generally speaking women make the best caregivers for children.

AGREE _____   DISAGREE _____

For the typical wife, her first desire is not for a career but for a home and family.

AGREE _____   DISAGREE _____

Comparing your answers to the above statements can provide much valuable sharing. If both of you are working, try to come to some mutual conclusions as to why you both work, how long this will continue, and where the children fit in.

9 Read the last two sections of Chapter Sixteen: "Have You Ever Said, 'Thanks for Working'?" and "He Wants a Woman Who Believes in Him" (book pages 200–03). Then take the True or False test that pertains to you:

Mark each statement T for True, or F for False.

_____ I have told my husband numerous times, "Thanks for working."

_____ I sometimes think my husband works too long and too much.

_____ My husband is much more than a "meal ticket" to me.

Mark each statement T or F.

___ It would be (is) nice to be told, "Thanks for working."

___ I know I work too many hours, but feel I have no choice.

___ I sometimes feel I'm just a "meal ticket."

 Compare your answers and discuss them. Be sensitive to each other, particularly concerning "working too many hours." Note Emerson's comment on page 202 of *Love & Respect*: "If he is a good-willed man who is neglecting his family by working too much, he will realize it, and you can talk it through and work it out." (For more on a man working too much see *Love & Respect* Appendix E, page 315.)

10 Go over the tips on book page 203 ("Your Husband Will Feel You Appreciate His Desire to Work and Achieve When . . ."). Choose two or three you think could benefit your marriage. When do you see these being tried?

 Compare notes on what each of you chose. If the husband's feelings about how his work is perceived did not come out in Question 5, they may be clearer as the two of you talk about it here.

A JOURNAL OF MY JOURNEY
TO LOVE AND RESPECT

You should be very comfortable at this point with recording your thoughts and impressions of your journey toward Love and Respect. Continue to follow through at the conclusion of each session until the end of the workbook.

Scripture Meditations

1. As you begin your study of C-H-A-I-R-S, remember that each letter in the acronym is designed to help the wife who may well be sailing in uncharted waters called "unconditional respect." Emerson has talked to many wives who want to respect their husbands unconditionally, but they are not sure how to go about it. To these wives I say, "How perfectly you do this is not the issue; how willing you are is what counts." A good verse to keep in mind is Proverbs 14:1: "The wise woman builds her house, but with her own hands the foolish one tears hers down" (NIV). One woman who had realized her mistakes wrote: "I am 'a nasty, big mouth wench' who emotionally abused her husband by her lack of respect and bad behavior. I know a foolish woman tears down her own house, now I want to build my house back up." Chances are you are not in this woman's shoes, but perhaps God is calling you to make some things right. What, specifically, can you start practicing as a way to respect your husband unconditionally?

2. The husband who finds a good spouse who supports, appreciates, and respects him "obtains favor from the LORD" (Proverbs 18:22). Have you ever heard your husband say, in one way or another, that he was a favored man because of you? If not, there are two possible reasons: he is overlooking the gift you are to him and needs to be more mature in his evaluation of you; or perhaps your disrespect has made it hard for him to feel and express his appreciation. Have you ever considered that you have been given by the Lord to your husband to meet his need to be respected? Has it occurred to you that this is part of God's call on your life? Is this call getting easier to answer? Why or why not?

My current thoughts about our marriage:

SESSION TEN

In preparation for this session, read Chapter Seventeen, "Hierarchy—Appreciate His Desire to Protect and Provide," and Chapter Eighteen, "Authority—Appreciate His Desire to Serve and to Lead." The following questions are for study by an individual or study by a couple. Spouses studying together should note that Chapters Seventeen and Eighteen cover material that is complex and sensitive. Leave plenty of time for reading and discussing all of the additional commentary as well as *Workbook* Appendix IV, which deals with mutual submission. Remember to answer all unmarked questions first, then answer questions marked by the male or female icon (whichever applies to you). Finally, answer the questions with the couple icon, if you're studying with your mate. (Suggestions for leading a small group in studying this workbook can be found in *Workbook* Appendix I, page 201.)

Questions for Chapter Seventeen

1 According to the dictionary, *hierarchy* means "a body of persons organized or classified according to rank, capacity, or authority." When you read the phrase, "hierarchy in marriage," what immediately comes to mind? Check the answer that comes closest to your honest first response, or write your own.

    ____ a. Politically incorrect.

    ____ b. Men think they are superior.

    ____ c. God's plan is good, but men abuse it.

    ____ d. I think:

Compare your answers. Did either of you check or write a definition that interprets "hierarchy in marriage" negatively? Discuss what Emerson says on page 205 of *Love & Respect*. Does he think the Bible supports chauvinism and the "superiority of the male"? Write down the gist of what you believe Emerson is saying:

2 According to the section "What Is the Real Meaning of 'Biblical Hierarchy'?" (book pages 206–8), what kind of hierarchy has God planned for marriage? (See also Ephesians 5:22–24.) What does God call the husband to do? What does He call the wife to do?

Talk about a husband's responsibility to love, protect, and provide for his wife. Take a second look together at the letter from a wife on book page 207. How did she first interpret her husband's firm, even a bit gruff, efforts to lead and protect her? What changed her mind about his leadership?

3 According to Emerson (book pages 207–8) an evil-willed man might abuse his position as head of the family but a good-willed man would not take advantage of his wife or children because "that is not his nature. He will not use his position as 'chair' of the family against those he is to love and protect."

 Do you think Emerson is right? How do you see your husband in his role as "head" of the family? Which statement comes closest to describing him? Or if you prefer, write your own:

___ a. I am comfortable with my husband as "head." He does a good job.

___ b. I agree he should be the "head," but I wish I could have more input.

___ c. I am not completely comfortable with my husband as "head." He thinks he is being biblical, but he puts the children and me down at times.

___ d. I think:

 How do you view your God-given position as "head" of the family? Which of the following statements best describes how you feel about having this responsibility?

___ a. Uncomfortable. I never asked to be the "head," but when I try to do what the Bible says, I don't get a lot of support from my family.

___ b. Comfortable. As far as I know I do not lord it over my wife and kids.

___ c. I'm willing to be "head," but I could use some help sometimes.

___ d. I think:

Compare what you checked or wrote: this could be a sensitive question, for either of you. Before discussing your answers, agree with God that you want to show each other love and respect. Both of you need to be humble and willing to accept feedback from each other, even if it smarts a bit. After (or perhaps during) your discussion, read together Emerson's additional commentary in *Workbook* Appendix VI to get additional input.

Following are some questions for a good-willed husband to help him evaluate how he feels when his wife chooses quietness rather than being verbally contentious. As a husband, which of the following comes closest to what you might think? (As a wife, which of the following would you say your husband would choose?)

____ a. Her quietness is an endorsement of my position and no further discussion is needed. I get what I want.

____ b. I'm afraid her quietness is short term and insincere; she will verbally attack me if she doesn't get her way.

____ c. Her quietness gets my attention and calms me down. I often feel convicted about where I have been unreasonable and want to make amends.

____ d. I think her quietness is one of two things: weakness and fear, or rebellion and anger. Either way, when she won't talk to me I get irritated.

____ e. Her quietness? That would be nice. I have not encountered what Emerson describes.

____ f. I think:

 This can be sensitive. Remember that both of you have goodwill and want to treat each other with love and respect. The good-willed wife may want to assure her husband that she never uses quietness as a ploy or a weapon. The good-willed husband may want to reassure his wife that as she seeks to obey God, he will seek to respond in good faith as well. (For more examples of how a wife's quiet respectfulness can influence her husband, go to http://www.love andrespect.com/pearl/)

———

4 Read "Paul Versus Today's Culture" (book pages 208–9). In an "ideal marriage relationship," how does a husband act? What are some reasons a wife might be hesitant to place herself under her husband as "the head"? Which of the following comments might apply to you and your spouse?

____ a. He can be the head, but will he really care about my needs?

____ b. I want him to be the head, but not too much.

____ c. What if headship becomes dictatorship?

____ d. I make more than he does, so why does he get to be the head?

____ e. My comment:

 Compare the answers you checked or wrote down. Is "the husband as head" an accepted concept in your marriage, or are there concerns and questions? At the bottom of book page 208 and top of 209, Emerson describes a problem many wives have (and that includes Christian spouses). They want to be treated like a princess but "deep down they resist treating their husbands like the king." Do you think he is right or wrong? Or, would you say this is true of some marriages but not yours?

———

5 In "How to Deflate a Husband with Seven Words" (book page 209), find the remark a wife made that deflated and disrespected her husband. Fill in the blanks:

"You need _____ _____ _____ _____ _____.**"**

Why would this remark hurt a husband so badly? List some reasons here:

Compare your answers and discuss what happened in the incident described on book pages 209–10. Was the husband too sensitive? Did the wife have any clue about what showing him respect might mean? In earlier sessions you covered the question that any Love and Respect spouse can ask to guard against being unloving or disrespectful. For husband or wife, the question begins: "Is what I am about to say or do . . . ." How does this question end for the husband? For the wife? (If you need help, see "Always ask yourself" in *Love & Respect* Appendix A, page 305.)

6 Read the touching story in "Showing Respect by Candlelight," book pages 210–11. What stands out in this account of how and why Dr. E. V. Hill and his wife, Jane, ate by candlelight? Write down your strongest impressions.

Compare your answers. Wife, if something like this would happen to you and your husband, would your natural response be similar to what Jane Hill did? Husband, if you found yourself in the same situation as Dr. Hill, how would you have responded to the "candlelight dinner for two"? Talk together about how important finances are to a marriage. Is Emerson correct in saying: "Mark it down. Men are more vulnerable to criticism when it is related to headship issues"?

7 Read "The Card He'll Keep Forever" (book pages 211–13). Why does being told by his wife that she respects his leadership work so powerfully on the typical husband? Write your own ideas. How do they compare with what the husband says in his letter on page 212?

 Compare your answers. This could possibly be an awkward question for one or both of you, so be sensitive to each other's feelings. (The use of a Respect Test or Respect Note was covered in Session 9, but it is well worth repeating here, in this session on hierarchy.) Wife, are you willing to write such a card or note to express appreciation for his leadership and protection? Husband, what would you think if she did? Would you save such a card or note to read and reread it?

8 Go over the tips in "Your Husband Will Feel You Appreciate His Desire to Protect and Provide When . . ." (book pages 213–14). Choose one or more that you believe would benefit your marriage. Write down your choices, putting them in your own words as much as possible, and adding ideas of your own that would apply.

Husbands should write down their choices too. Compare the ideas each of you chose and then agree on at least one thing the wife can do or practice during the coming week. At the end of the week, talk together about how it went for each of you. Is it worth continuing? What other ideas could you try?

Questions for Chapter Eighteen

9 Read "Who's the Boss at Your House?" (book pages 216–17). Then indicate whether you agree or disagree with the following statements and write a brief reason for your answer.

a. Men and women are totally equal, and husbands don't have any more responsibility and authority than their wives do.

AGREE ___   DISAGREE ___   **Explain:**

b. The good-willed husband who acts responsibly and lovingly as leader of his home always works out compromises that are mutually pleasing.

AGREE ____   DISAGREE ____   **Explain:**

c. If a wife is a better decision maker and has better judgment than her husband, she should demand equal say regarding what they buy, where they go, what they do.

AGREE ____   DISAGREE ____   **Explain:**

d. The good-willed wife who is more competent than her husband needs to demonstrate her abilities by her respectful speech and deferential attitude, with the confidence that in time her husband will prize her giftedness.

AGREE ____   DISAGREE ____   **Explain:**

 Compare your answers to these statements. This could be a sensitive area, particularly if the wife is inclined toward the feminist view, which claims that men and women should have equal authority and responsibility. A good goal is not to cater to what society and culture are saying about husbands and wives but work to understand what Scripture says. Many wives are like the young woman in the opening of Chapter Eighteen (book page 215) who said: "I want him to be the head. I want him to be the leader. I just want to make sure that he makes decisions in keeping with what I want."

10 Read "Does Scripture Teach Mutual Submission?" (book pages 217–19), where Emerson discusses the concept of "mutual submission" which says husbands and wives should submit to one another with neither one being owed any special deference. What impressions or opinions do you have about "mutual submission?" Choose from the statements on the next page, or write your own assessment.

___ a. Mutual submission sounds unworkable. Ultimately, someone has to be responsibly in charge.

___ b. These mutual submission people may have something. I need to get more info.

___ c. I prefer the Love and Respect approach.

___ d. I think:

As you compare your answers, be aware that for some couples this could be a sensitive question. Biblical feminists have argued in recent years for a certain kind of "mutual submission," which they base on Ephesians 5:21: "Submit to one another out of reverence for Christ" (NIV). Those proposing this particular mutual submission approach interpret Ephesians 5:21 to mean that the wife owes no special submission to her husband. However, Ephesians 5:22 clearly says: "Wives, submit to your husbands as to the Lord" (NIV). The Love and Respect approach to marriage is based on Ephesians 5:22, which does not give a husband a mandate to treat his wife poorly. On the contrary, he is to defer to his wife's need for love in all situations. This is his goal, even though he is certain to fall short at times. Review page 218 of *Love & Respect*, especially the discussion of how to deal with honest stalemates. For more on mutual submission and a detailed explanation of the apparent contradiction in Ephesians 5:21–22, see *Workbook* Appendix IV, page 213.

11 Read "Husbands Are Responsible to 'Make the Call'" (book pages 219–21). How does a Love and Respect couple reach a decision when there is an honest stalemate, a difference of opinion where husband and wife both have good points and reasons why they believe their way is best? List some steps they can take to keep Love and Respect working in their relationship. According to book page 220, if the husband has to "make the call" and his wife does not agree with it, how does she cope with the temptation to feel unloved at the moment? How does she show him respect?

 Compare your answers and talk about how you deal with stalemates in your own marriage. Wife, do you agree with Emerson's advice on book page 220 to remain respectful and quiet? Husband, do you accept your responsibility to "make the call" when necessary if a decision is needed and you can't agree with each other? For additional help with your discussion, see *Workbook* Appendix IV, as well as Emerson's additional commentary in *Workbook* Appendix VI.

---

12 The following paragraphs are excerpted from the section in "Authority Must Come with Responsibility" (book pages 221–23). Mark your reaction to each paragraph and put down a brief reason why.

a. ". . . because God has made your husband responsible (review Ephesians 5:25–33), he needs the authority to carry out that responsibility. No smoothly running organization can have two heads. To set up a marriage with two equals at the head is to set it up for failure. . . . God knew someone had to be in charge, and that is why Scripture teaches that, in order for things to work, the wife is called to defer to her husband."

AGREE ___ DISAGREE ___ **Explain:**

b. "If you want to work with your husband to reach mutually satisfying decisions most of the time, follow this principle: GO ON RECORD WITH YOUR HUSBAND THAT YOU SEE HIM AS HAVING 51 PERCENT OF THE RESPONSIBILITY AND, THERE-FORE, 51 PERCENT OF THE AUTHORITY. Once you go on record about his author-ity, he will not feel you are trying to be the boss. As you submit (which simply means recognizing his biblically given authority), you will not be a doormat. In fact, you will get your way far more often than you would if you 'stood up for your rights,' which usually means being disrespectful."

AGREE ___   DISAGREE ___   **Explain:**

c. ". . . among good-willed couples, if there are one hundred decisions over a three-month period related to the family, the wife will have a strong opinion on ninety-nine of them, and her opinion will usually be respected and have strong influence."

AGREE ___   DISAGREE ___   **Explain:**

For spouses studying together: compare your answers and discuss as many as possible. If you have definite disagreement on a certain paragraph, you may want to focus on that. For additional discussion ideas, see the additional commentary in *Workbook* Appendix VI. (For more on how a wife's submission can strengthen a marriage, see *Workbook* Appendix IV.)

———————

13 Look over the tips in "He Will Feel You Appreciate His Authority and Leadership When . . ." (book pages 224–25) and choose one or more that sound useful for your marriage. Here and on the next page write down what you have chosen, and start thinking of how this idea might be carried out.

Compare your choices. Discuss why you think these particular ideas are important. Be sure the husband gives his input on what he would like his wife to try.

A JOURNAL OF MY JOURNEY
TO LOVE AND RESPECT

Write your responses to any Scripture Meditations that seem to speak especially to your regarding your marriage. Also, put down something, no matter how brief, about your current feelings, fears, or questions.

SCRIPTURE MEDITATIONS

1. "Those who talk a lot are likely to sin. But those who control their tongues are wise" (Proverbs 10:19 NIRV). Some wives feel nothing can be resolved apart from talking. Proverbs 10:19, however, says that sometimes too much talk ends up in sin. This is especially true because of the thoughts that precede the talk, as one wife discovered. She wrote to me to say she had begun to realize the many ways she had been disrespectful to her husband during twenty-six years of marriage. The result was she didn't have the marriage she would have liked and she began asking God to alert her when she was going to say something disrespectful. At first she couldn't recognize the disrespect until after it was out of her mouth, but then she began recognizing the disrespectful words as they were going through her mind and realized they could be stopped. It also helped to hear her pastor preach on the need to control the tongue, that what comes out of our mouths is what we put in our hearts. Her letter concludes: "If we feed on God's Word, that is what comes out of our mouths; likewise I recognized that if we feed on being irritated with our husbands, thinking about how they fail us, hurt, or offend us, that is what comes out of our mouths . . . . Luke 6:45 says, 'What's stored

up in the heart overflows in the mouth.' (That may be paraphrased.) Sounds like love and respect to me!"

2. A wife's willingness to show her husband respect and defer to his authority should not undermine her God-given abilities, as the Proverbs 31 woman clearly demonstrates: "She considers a field and buys it; from her earnings she plants a vineyard" (Proverbs 31:16). As a husband, have you considered designating authority to your wife in certain areas, which will empower her to use her God-given talents? I have done so in my marriage, with wonderful results. My wife, Sarah, is an efficient administrator when it comes to finances. I have entrusted her with the day-to-day bills and financial decisions because I trust her heart and competencies. I am grateful to God, because this has freed me to focus my abilities elsewhere. Why has this worked? One reason is that Sarah has never been afraid to communicate to me that she sees me as the one having 51 percent authority. Another reason is that I have never feared designating the day-to-day authority to her for the finances. She looks to me for approval and sanctioning when new and more major questions arise, and I ask for her counsel as we come to a final decision. In our case this has worked beautifully. I feel respected as the one who is ultimately responsible, but I give her the authority as the one who is immediately involved.

My current thoughts about our marriage:

SESSION ELEVEN

In preparation for this session, read Chapter Nineteen, "Insight—Appreciate His Desire to Analyze and Counsel." The following questions are for individual study or study by a couple. Remember to answer all unmarked questions first, then answer questions marked by the male or female icon (whichever applies to you). Finally, answer the questions with the couple icon, if you're studying with your mate. (Suggestions for leading a small group in studying this workbook can be found in *Workbook* Appendix I, page 201.)

Questions for Chapter Nineteen

1 On the opening pages of Chapter Nineteen, read the story of the wife who decides to visit her husband where he works. What does she see? What does she learn? What has she been missing?

Compare the notes you made with what your mate discovered. Did you see the same things? Where did you differ? Discuss the story to see if it has any relevance to your marriage. If it does, be sensitive to each other and express your ideas with the "Is what I'm about to say or do . . ." question in mind. (See *Love & Respect* Appendix A, page 305.) Analyze together the letter from the wife at the bottom of book pages 228–29. Has either one of you thought much about the importance of a man's insight? How would you rate your typical daily exchanges? Are they conversations or monologues?

—————

2 In "I No Longer Believe Totally in Womanly Intuition," book page 229, Emerson admits he no longer gives complete credence to two beliefs he once held: (1) that the vast majority of men are opinionated, one-sided, and inattentive; and (2) that women possess an exclusive and unique power of intuition that is always right. Why did he change his mind? Check the answer that fits or write your own thoughts:

____ a. He realized he was getting a very one-sided view from the wives he counseled.

____ b. He read some helpful books that straightened him out.

____ c. He realized that constantly pounding on men to "listen to the intuition of your wives. . . . God will teach you through your wives" was tipping the scales too much.

____ d. My thoughts:

The correct answer to the quiz above is obvious, but one or both of you may have written something you want to discuss. Why did Emerson change his mind after twenty years of thinking one certain way about men and women? Is he saying he no longer believes at all in "womanly intuition"?

3 Read book page 230, "It Was Eve, Not Adam, Who Was Deceived." How does Genesis 3:1–6 show that wives should never feel they need to be ready with all the answers and do all the thinking? Is Emerson saying that Eve was responsible for the Fall? What part did both of them play in the Fall? Read Romans 5:12–21. Who does Paul name as primarily responsible?

Compare your notes with your mate's. What is Emerson's point in bringing up the account from Genesis 3? Is he trying to put down women? How does 1 Timothy 2:14 shed light on the discussion? Talk about the fact that neither of you is infallible; you both have equal weight to pull in family decisions. How would you rate yourselves in this area?

____ a. Both give input on decisions.

_____ b. Wife has much more to say and do regarding the family.

_____ c. Husband makes most of the decisions.

_____ d. My comments:

⎯⎯⎯⎯⎯⎯

4 In "A Marriage Needs Her Intuition and His Insight" (book pages 231–34), Emerson mentions an area where he believes some women are deceiving themselves today: their criticism of their husbands for lack of spiritual leadership in the family. Analyze the letters from two wives (bottom of page 231) who are distressed because their husbands are not what they would like them to be regarding spiritual matters. To women with this kind of problem, Emerson says: "Your convictions can please God, but your contempt can also grieve Him." What does Emerson go on to say to wives whose husbands do not appear to be spiritual giants? What does he suggest that these wives do—and not do?

 The problem of "lack of spiritual leadership by the husband" may or may not apply to your marriage. As a husband, if you are taking spiritual leadership, rejoice with your wife in that fact. As a wife, if you wish your husband would take more spiritual leadership, first ask him if he would mind discussing this. If he is open, proceed to explain what you wish the two of you could work out in matters such as family devotions, praying together, and church life. (For additional discussion material on the husband's spiritual leadership, see Emerson's commentary in *Workbook* Appendix VI.)

(For more on how a wife can help her husband, see Question 5 below. And for more on the husband's spiritual leadership go to http://www.loveandrespect.com/pearl/)

5 At the bottom of book page 232, Emerson lists some questions for the wife to ask herself about any area of leadership where she feels her husband's leadership is lacking or questionable. Which of these questions, if any, apply to your marriage? Write them here:

Also, read the rest of page 233 and most of page 234, down to the next subhead. Do any of the following statements by Emerson from these pages apply to your marriage at all?

    ____ a. ". . . ask yourself if you may possibly have an attitude of self-righteousness —at least to some degree. . . . You may well believe, as many women do, that you are a better person than he is and that he needs to change."

My thoughts on this:

___ b. "What I see happening in some marriages is that the wife believes—or appears to believe—that she does not sin. In many other marriages the only sin that a wife will readily admit to is her negative reaction to her husband's failure to be loving or for losing patience with the children."

My thoughts on this:

___ c. ". . . it's easy for a wife to discount or disparage a husband's suggestion that she has some problem that needs correcting. Even if he is gentle and diplomatic in suggesting that she needs to make a correction . . . he is quickly silenced. She is offended, wounded, and angered by his assessment. He is accused of being without understanding and compassion. He has no right to speak. And he will often wind up being shown contempt."

My thoughts on this:

Be sensitive to each other as you share your thoughts on these statements, which are quite confrontational to the wife. None of them may apply in your marriage, and if so, celebrate this fact together. If something does apply to some degree, discuss it calmly, always invoking the "Is what I am about to say . . . " rule (see *Love & Respect* Appendix A, book page 305). You may not be able to agree on every point, but try to follow Emerson's advice: "I believe husband and wife together need to examine any situation where something is amiss and try to come to a solution or, if needed, seek godly counsel."

6 In "Are You Trying to Be Your Husband's Holy Spirit?" (book page 234–237), Emerson warns that in many marriages, wives see their husbands as unrighteous. He writes, "Because she is the one who constantly seems to have to be on top of things, such as correcting the children (and him), she slips into an attitude of self-righteousness without realizing it. It is often subconscious, but a subtle judgmental spirit comes over a woman. Many women have admitted to me, 'I've got to stop being my husband's Holy Spirit.' . . . I never hear men saying, 'I've got to stop being my wife's Holy Spirit.'" How can a wife avoid slipping into a judgmental attitude (even though she may have good reason)? See especially pages 235–36 for practical ideas and list them here.

This can be another sensitive question, so walk softly to avoid stepping on each other's air hose. On book page 235, Emerson cites the account of Mary and Martha (Luke 10:38–42), which contains wisdom that is equally good for husbands and wives. Humbly focusing on Christ is a good way to avoid being or sounding judgmental. To paraphrase Jesus, "Don't look for the speck in your spouse's eye, be aware of the possible log in your own!" (see Matthew 7:1–5). Talk together about what this section may be saying to one or both of you. Note the wife's letter, bottom of page 236, top of 237, for more good advice.

7 Check the tips under "Your Husband Will Feel You Appreciate His Insight and Counsel When . . ." (book page 237). Choose one or more that look applicable for you and write them here for reference later. (Note how many of these tips parallel tips under Understanding, in Chapter Eleven. A husband is a natural-born

"fixer," so in some cases you may have to accept his insight, when all you think you need is his listening ear.)

 Compare notes on what you chose. As a wife, it might be especially appropriate in this instance to ask for your husband's insight. Which ideas did he choose? What does he want you to do first?

A Journal of My Journey
to Love and Respect

Write any thoughts prompted by the following Scripture Meditations by Emerson, or just record your perception of how the study has gone to this point.

Scripture Meditations

1. Proverbs 3:7 tells us, "Do not be wise in your own eyes. . . ." This warning is often applied to men, who can be very firm about their view of things. But doesn't this verse

apply to women as well? For instance, a group of wives may gather for coffee, even Bible study, and wind up talking about their marriages and how their husbands "just don't get it." The implication: the wife always "gets it" regarding what God had in mind with creation of male and female. Yes, the wife certainly has her very pink point of view, but does she really "get it" regarding the very blue point of view of her husband? "Do not be wise in your own eyes" cuts both ways. Husband and wife both need to adjust their sunglasses and hearing aids and become wise together as they seek God's counsel.

2. I have counseled many wives who admit that, deep down, they consider themselves better than their husbands—at least "better" in the sense of how to love the family and run the household. It is not hard to see why a wife may feel this way, but she should be aware that this is a dangerous state of mind. Listen to Paul's words in I Timothy 2:14: "Adam was not the one deceived; it was the woman who was deceived and became a sinner" (NIV). Paul isn't letting Adam off the hook. He followed as his wife lead him like a lamb to the slaughter and wound up being held responsible for the Fall (see Romans 5:12–19). The point is, husbands and wives are both sinners; both face their own private temptations. In 1 Timothy 2:14 Paul reminds today's wife that Eve was the one who was deceived (and by implication, so can she be deceived). When a woman, for whatever good reasons, begins to think she is intrinsically better than her husband, she slips into being self-righteous and judgmental (all in a "loving way," of course). To those who might say or even think, "I am holier than you," God replies that this kind of attitude is "smoke in My nostrils, a fire that burns all the day" (see Isaiah 65:5). First Timothy 2:14 is not there to shame the wife but to remind her she can be deceived. She must ask herself, "Am I a better person because God made me one way and my spouse another? Can either of us be saved apart from Jesus and His grace?" These questions are equally good for the husband. They enable husband and wife to come together in mutual confession and joyful connection.

3. As a wife, are you looking for ways to make it easier for your husband to lead and give insight? Peter has a lovely thought in 1 Peter 3. He says your real beauty "should be that of your inner self, the unfading beauty of a gentle and quiet spirit, which is of great worth in God's sight" (1 Peter 3:4 NIV). As you get dressed for the day, it is

important to look well-groomed, fresh, and attractive on the outside, but the more important thing is what is inside. A good daily prayer might be: "Lord, as I dress this morning, please clothe me in a gentle and quiet spirit."

My current thoughts about our marriage:

SESSION TWELVE

In preparation for this session, read Chapter Twenty, "Relationship—Appreciate His Desire for Shoulder-to-Shoulder Friendship" Chapter Twenty-one, "Sexuality—Appreciate His Desire for Sexual Intimacy," and Chapter Twenty-two, "The Energizing Cycle Will Work If You Do." The following questions are for an individual or a husband and wife studying together. Remember to answer all unmarked questions first, then answer questions marked by the male or female icon (whichever applies to you). Finally, answer the questions with the couple icon, if you're studying with your mate. (Suggestions for anyone planning to use this workbook with a small group can be found in *Workbook* Appendix I, page 201.)

Questions for Chapter Twenty

1 Read book pages 239–40 in *Love & Respect*. Is your marriage anything like the marriage described in the opening of Chapter Twenty? In your marriage, does he just want her to "be with him" with little or no talking? Check the answer that comes closest to describing you and your spouse.

OFTEN THE CASE ___   SELDOM HAPPENS ___   NEVER HAPPENS ___

My comments:

Discuss how much shoulder-to-shoulder activity you engage in with little or no talking. Emerson has seen this phenomenon in many couples over the years, but not necessarily everyone. Wife, if your husband does ask you to "just sit with him" from time to time, do you do it? Does it cause any problems if he wants to do little or no talking while he watches the news or his favorite program, reads a book or the paper, or works on a project or a hobby? Husband, if you have never engaged in shoulder-to-shoulder activity with your wife without talking, would you like to try it? What would she say if you did?

This session can take the two of you in three possible directions: (1) the wife will learn a new way to meet a basic need in her husband for shoulder-to-shoulder activity; (2) you both will better understand why he needs this kind of activity and why it energizes him; or (3) you both will agree he doesn't need shoulder-to-shoulder much, if at all.

2 Read "How Can 'Doing Nothing' Build a Relationship?" (book pages 240–42). What are some reasons a wife might have trouble with just sitting with her husband watching TV or watching him work on a project in his workshop? How does this need in many husbands illustrate major differences between "pink" (wives) and "blue" (husbands)?

Compare your answers, then discuss them. The typical wife could have real problems with just sitting "doing nothing" when she has so many chores and other activities. But would it be worth the time if it leads to feeling closer as a couple—and, possibly later, face-to-face talking?

---

3 In "For a While There, Sarah Wasn't Friendly" (book pages 242–43), Emerson recounts a time when Sarah was not too friendly, not only toward him, but the rest of the family in general. Her cleanliness standards were being violated, and she was always on everyone to pick up, wash up, and shape up. What happened to change Sarah's mind?

Talk about this story together. Here, indeed, was a case of "pink" and "blue" needing to like each other in spite of weaknesses and faults. Go back to the top of book page 242. Talk about how husbands and wives need to be lovers, yes, but also shoulder-to-shoulder friends. In Song of Solomon 5:10–16, the wife describes her husband in the most amorous of terms, but she also adds, "This is my beloved and this is my friend" (vs. 16).

---

4 Read the section under "Wives, Be Patient with 'Just Sit by Me'" (book pages 243–45). Which of the following sentences or paragraphs excerpted from this section give you insights into the male need to just be "shoulder-to-shoulder" with little or no talking?

    ____ a. "When the husband calls the wife in to 'just sit by him,' he is working on their relationship in a significant way. . . . This is the way a husband communicates."

_____ b. "Males prefer shoulder-to-shoulder communication instead of face-to-face communication, and this can occur in the simplest of ways."

_____ c. "In most marriages, then, there is a real difference in basic needs. As we saw in Chapter Nine, she wants to talk, to be close. But in this chapter we see that the natural bent of the male is to be shoulder-to-shoulder with a lot less talking. Obviously, there must be some give and take at this point as there should be in so many other areas of marriage."

Regarding "shoulder-to-shoulder with little talking" I think:

Compare any notes you have made concerning choices *a*, *b*, or *c* above. As mentioned earlier, not all husbands have this need, but many do. If shoulder-to-shoulder is something he wants to do, how can his need be balanced with her need to be close and just talk?

5 Read the experiences of three different wives in "Spend Time Together, Stay Together" (book pages 246–47). What can be learned from the wife in Peoria? From the letters by wives who are benefiting from being shoulder-to-shoulder? Write down any key words or phrases you find.

Compare notes on what you found in these accounts. And be sure to discuss the last two paragraphs in this section. Does Emerson's "twelve-week experiment" sound worth trying? Is it too much to ask a wife to do something that feels unnatural? Are the possible benefits worth it?

6 Go over the tips in "Your Husband Will Feel You Value His Shoulder-to-Shoulder Friendship When . . ." (book pages 247–48). Which of these might benefit your marriage? Write them here, with any added notes on how they can best be implemented.

Compare your choices and decide on what should be tried first. After a week or so, compare notes on how it is going. Make adjustments, if any are needed.

Questions for Chapter Twenty-One

7 Read the opening story of the doctor and his wife, plus the section called "They Kicked the Devil out of Bed" (book pages 249–51). How did the doctor's wife turn their impasse into a win-win?

Which of the following statements from this section speak most directly to you and your marriage?

    ___ a. "If there ever were an issue that isn't really the issue, it is sex."

    ___ b. "Sex for him and affection for you is a two-way street."

    ___ c. "Sex is symbolic of his deeper need—respect."

Complete this sentence: In our marriage, sex is . . .

 There is a lot to compare and talk about in Question 7 that could lead to tension. Much depends on how satisfying your sex life as a couple is at the moment. Ideally, husband and wife meet each other's major needs: his for sex, hers for intimacy through affection mixed with plenty of talking. Then both are content. But often there is an imbalance that leads to friction and fighting or a dull and boring relationship. Be sensitive to each other as you talk through this three-part question. If he doesn't think he gets enough sex, or she doesn't think she gets enough affection and closeness with talking, do not condemn one another. Share what you can, always seeking to show each other love and respect. (For more ideas and suggestions, see *Workbook* Appendix V, "Sex: Love and Respect Come First—Then, 'Just Do It!'"(page 218).

8 Read "Two Keys to Understanding Your Husband" (book pages 251–53). Emerson describes two aspects of why a husband has sexual desire for his wife. What are they? Put each one in a sentence or two at the most.

 On book page 252 is a story about a mother who gives her daughter some advice concerning sex. Do you agree or disagree (explain your choice) with her when she says, "Why would you deprive him of something that takes such a short amount of time and makes him soooooo happy"?

AGREE ____   DISAGREE ____

Compare your answers to the two aspects of a man's sexual desire for his wife. Put in its simplest terms: he sees her and he wants her. If she wants him, she can make him sooooo happy. But it isn't always that simple, as most couples can attest. Talk about how the husband needs to woo his wife with close-ness, openness, and sincerely talking with her to connect with her. When the wife feels close, she may want to become close physically, but it is an interplay that both spouses must work out in terms that are unique to their relationship. As always, this kind of interplay should be governed by love and respect.

9 In "The Golden Rule Works with Sex Too" (book page 253), Emerson describes the tension in every marital sexual relationship. She wants to feel close emotionally in order to connect sexually. He wants to feel close sexually in order to connect emotionally. Neither is wrong, just different. In the second paragraph in this section is a rule (see line in italics) that applies to every principle covered in the Energizing Cycle, and especially sexuality. This rule, which never changes, is (copy it here and commit it to memory):

Talk together about the rule that never changes. Are you at a point where you are getting better at sharing your needs with each other openly, with-out stepping on each other's air hose? This could be a good time to review together *Love & Respect* Appendix C: "How to Ask Your Mate to Meet Your Needs" (see page 311–312). See especially what she can say about closeness and openness, and what he can say about sexuality. Obviously, these "scripted statements" are only sug-gestions. Each spouse can and should work out her or his own way of communicating needs to the other.

10 "A Dose of Respect Beats a Dose of Viagra Any Day" (book pages 254–55) includes two letters, one from a wife whose husband committed adultery, and one from a husband who also strayed. In both cases, why was the husband vulnerable to infidelity? What does this say about the link between sex and respect?

Share your answers, which may or may not be similar. In both cases the husbands were being deprived of sex, but the thing that really drew each man into an adulterous relationship and held him there was that his adulterous partner made him feel admired and respected. As one of the straying husbands wrote, "Somebody thought I was okay." What does this say about the constant need to let each other know, "You are okay, lovable, respectable, wanted, and needed"? Are these positives being communicated in your marriage?

11 Read "If He Loves Me, How Can He Be Tempted by Other Women?" (book pages 255–58). Which of the following statements, taken from the paragraphs near the bottom of page 257 and top of 258, are most helpful to you as a spouse? Add your comments below.

____ a. "A man is responsive to what he sees. He needs his wife's understanding of his struggles. If he wanted to be untrue to her, he would never allude to the problem at all."

____ b. "A wife longs to receive her husband's closeness, openness, and understanding. You can achieve this in two ways: (1) do your best to give him the sexual release he needs, even if on some occasions you aren't in the mood, or (2) let him know you are trying to comprehend that he is tempted sexually in ways you don't understand."

____ c. "If your husband is typical, he has a need you don't have. When you shame him, punish him, or deprive him, he feels dishonored for who he is. . . . But he needs you. . . . As you recognize his need and seek to meet it, you will find him, reaching out to meet yours."

My comments on the quote I chose:

Compare your choice of quotes, realizing this can be a very sensitive subject. You may want to discuss one or more of the quotes above, or you may want to come back to this at another time. One solution for this problem that has worked for some couples is for the husband to meet with other men and share with them. In this way they can encourage each other to resist sexual temptation, as well as keep each other accountable.

12 Choose from the tips under "He Will Feel You Appreciate His Desire for Sexual Intimacy When . . ." (book page 258) and choose one that you believe can benefit your marriage. Write it down, with an estimated date for when it could be tried.

Compare notes and talk about how the two of you can make this happen. The husband should not put the entire burden on his wife. This is definitely a time for love on his part, respect on hers.

Questions for Chapter Twenty-Two

13 You have covered C-O-U-P-L-E and C-H-A-I-R-S, which give the husband and wife six ways each to love and respect each other. On book page 259 is the definition of the Energizing Cycle: His love _____ her _____. Her respect _____ his _____.

If you haven't memorized this yet, do it now, and never forget it. The Energizing Cycle is the answer to keeping the Crazy Cycle from turning on.

Now go to page 260. In "How Does a Husband Spell Love to His Wife?" is a brief review of C-O-U-P-L-E, six tools the husband can use to maintain his side of the Energizing Cycle for his marriage. If you are a husband, make some notes below on which of these six tools you have understood in a new way or even learned about for the first time. Which ones are easiest for you to use? Which ones are harder? Which ones have made a definite difference in your relationship? If you are a wife, make notes below on the six tools in C-O-U-P-L-E. Which ones has your husband been using? Which ones would you like to see him use more? Why?

Compare what you wrote. What does the husband think he has been doing well? Where does he see he could be doing better? What does the wife think he has been doing well? If the wife has suggestions on what the husband could be doing better or more often, she should be encouraging, not negative and complaining. The point is, even small steps of progress on the Energizing Cycle are symbolic of a big step of progress for your marriage.

---

14 "How Does a Wife Spell Respect for Her Husband?" (book pages 260–61) is a brief review of C-H-A-I-R-S, six tools a wife can use to maintain her side of the Energizing Cycle for her marriage. If you are a wife, make some notes below on which of these six tools you have understood in a new way, or even learned about for the first time. Which ones are easiest for you to use? Which ones are harder? Has using any of these tools made a real difference in your relationship to your husband? In what way? If you are a husband, make notes below on the six tools in C-H-A-I-R-S. Which ones has your wife been using? Which ones would you like to see her use more? Why?

Compare your answers. What does the wife think she has been doing well? What does she think she could be doing better? What does the husband think she has been doing well? If the husband has some suggestions on what his wife could do better, he should be encouraging, not complaining (or even teasing).

15 Is it easy or hard to "cut your spouse some slack" as he or she tries to practice the principles in C-O-U-P-L-E or C-H-A-I-R-S? Read the wife's letter that begins on book page 261. What has she learned that all spouses should try to practice?

Compare your answers to see if you both included what the wife said about what her "first response" should be. To put it briefly: always try to find positives about your spouse, not negatives. This is not easy. The negative comes naturally. The positive is often much harder, because, look, your spouse has stepped on your air hose again!

On page 262 Emerson writes, "You can't grasp the Holy Grail of perfection, which is always beyond your reach. But you can embrace Love and Respect, which will always provide more than enough to energize your marriage." Is he right? Do you believe enough to act on the principles embodied in C-O-U-P-L-E and C-H-A-I-R-S? If you do, your marriage will not only be less negative and more positive, it will be the kind of marriage that honors Christ in every way. (To look ahead to the Rewarded Cycle, Part III, see "From the Energizing Cycle to the Rewarded Cycle" (pages 262–63.)

A Journal of My Journey to Love and Respect

Emerson's Scripture Meditations, below, are one possible source of journal entries you may want to make. Or just write your thoughts on where you are in your marriage. What do you see happening? What do you need to do or stop doing?

Scripture Meditations

1. A woman should consider how to be a companion to her husband. After all, God did say, "I will make a helper who is just right for him" (Genesis 2:18 NIRV). Have you, as a wife, considered that a most helpful activity for you that is just right for your husband is a shoulder-to-shoulder activity? Many husbands are energized by a wife's mere presence. As your husband's helper, have you been overlooking a very fruitful way to help your husband and energize your marriage?

2. In marriage, timing is everything. There is, indeed, "A time to be silent, and a time to speak" (Ecclesiastes 3:7). Have you seriously considered that there are times when talking is not a good thing? For example, if a husband has been unloving or disobedient to Christ in some other way, the shoulder-to-shoulder wife can find new meaning in "won without a word" (1 Peter 3:1). Although "without a word" may make little sense to you as a woman, God's Word is worth trusting. In the past, how persuaded have you been that the only way to convict your husband was by voicing your complaint to him? During this "season" of your marriage, is it a time to be silent? Could it be that when you are respectfully silent a husband can better listen to God and his own conscience?

3. "Your two breasts are like two fawns . . . that browse among the lilies" (Song of Solomon 4:5 NIV). This passage is describing the attraction a wife's breasts have for her visually oriented husband. When you courted, were you aware of his visual orientation?

Now that you are married, do you still acknowledge that orientation, or do you act as though it should not be there? What about your emotional orientation? Should he act as though it should not be there? If a husband denies his wife's emotional orientation, what could happen? If a wife denies her husband sexually, what could happen? For rather explicit details on how not to deny each other's needs, read Song of Solomon 4:1–15, which is Solomon's song of praise to his wife's charms. Also note verse 16, where the wife gives her husband a passionate invitation to be sexually intimate.

4. "With her flattering lips she seduced him" (Proverbs 7:21 NKJV). It is possible that a husband might be seduced by a sexy, sensual woman, but he is far more likely to be seduced by an admiring woman. We could assume the woman spoken of in Proverbs 7:21 flattered her victim with false respect and phony admiration. Actually, what she said to him could have been true enough, but her motives were false and manipulative. Why was he so easily manipulated? A good guess is that he could have been living with a wife who never said anything respectful to him, much less admiring.[i] When the adulteress laid her trap (see Proverbs 7:6–20), he fell for it completely, just as a wife who gets no emotional intimacy can be seduced by a man who is "kind and understanding." How can you affair-proof your marriage? With love, respect, and trust in God.

My current thoughts about our marriage:

[i] In Proverbs 7, the instruction is given to a "son" to avoid sexual temptation. Is this "son" married or unmarried? The answer is found earlier in Proverbs 5, where "sons" are exhorted to steer clear of sexual temptation (see v. 7 ff.). Some of these "sons" are married, according to Proverbs 5:18–19: "Let your fountain be blessed, and rejoice in the wife of your youth. As a loving hind and a graceful doe, let her breasts satisfy you at all times; be exhilarated always with her love."

PART THREE:
THE REWARDED CYCLE

Sessions 13 and 14 cover Chapters Twenty-three and Twenty-four, and the Conclusion of *Love & Respect*

A PERSONAL WORD FROM EMERSON:

In Part One you learned how to slow and stop the Crazy Cycle. In Part Two you learned how to build a better marriage with the Energizing Cycle. In Part Three the message is different and has multiple applications: the Rewarded Cycle is for couples who are trying the Love and Respect Connection but it isn't working well. They have slowed the Crazy Cycle but aren't quite on the Energizing Cycle. The Rewarded Cycle is also for spouses hanging on by a thread in a marriage where his unconditional love for her, or her unconditional respect for him, is getting little or no results. And finally, the Rewarded Cycle is for all couples who want to know the real reason for love and respect.

Ultimately, all husbands and wives should be practicing Love and Respect principles first and foremost out of obedience to Christ. If they do not, it is so easy to start being arrogantly proud about "our great marriage." So many marriages seem to be getting along just great, and then *wham*!—the wheels come off. If we take our eyes off Christ (or never put our eyes on Christ in the first place), we are building on sand, and when the storms come, we can be swept away (see Matthew 7:24–27).

What follows contains comfort, encouragement, and plenty of straight talk for any spouse who wants to learn the deepest meaning of respecting or loving unconditionally. The Rewarded Cycle explains that you love and respect, not because you want to save your marriage, or even strengthen your marriage (worthwhile as those goals are). You love and respect because you want to love and reverence Christ. In the ultimate sense, your marriage has nothing to do with your spouse. It has everything to do with your relationship to your Savior and Lord, and how much you want to serve and glorify Him.

SESSION THIRTEEN

In preparation for this session, read Chapter Twenty-three, "The Real Reason to Love and Respect." The following questions are for an individual or a husband and wife studying together. The suggestions for spouses studying together are of two kinds: (1) for couples who have managed to slow the Crazy Cycle, but are struggling to get on the Energizing Cycle; (2) for couples who are on the Energizing Cycle, but who can still profit from what the Rewarded Cycle has to tell them about how central Jesus Christ should be in a marriage. Remember to answer all unmarked questions first, then answer questions marked by the male or female icon (whichever applies to you). Finally, answer the questions with the couple icon, if you're studying with your mate. (Suggestions for anyone planning to use this *workbook* with a small group can be found in *Workbook* Appendix I, page 201.)

1 Read "Don't Give Up—Trust God to Work" (book pages 268–70). If you are a spouse who is struggling, which of the following quotes from this section speak to you the loudest right now?

    ___ a. "Don't give up just because it doesn't seem to be working."

    ___ b. "Don't doubt the light from God's Word in your dark times."

    ___ c. "Most often, Love or Respect is working on your spouse more than you realize."

    ___ d. "Have confidence that God will work."

Write your thoughts here and on the next page regarding what you checked above. How can one or more of these ideas help you right now?

If you have slowed the Crazy Cycle but can't seem to get the Energizing Cycle started in your marriage, look at the quotes above. If you haven't already checked one or more of them, do so now. Then, if both of you are willing, talk about where you are now and how you must trust God and His Word to work in your lives. (If yours is a marriage that is on the Energizing Cycle, rejoice together and give God the glory for what He has done, and what He will continue to do as you trust in Him.)

2 In "When It Simply Doesn't Work—What Then?" (book pages 270–71), Emerson explains what the Rewarded Cycle is all about. Following are some key quotes to consider if you have been ready to say, "This Love and Respect thing just doesn't work." Choose one of Emerson's statements and write some reasons why it encourages or enlightens you regarding your situation.

___ a. "When you love or respect unconditionally, you are following God and His will for you. Ultimately, your spouse and your marriage have nothing to do with it."

___ b. "Unconditional love and unconditional respect will be rewarded. I call this the Rewarded Cycle."

___ c. "I believe Paul also had your marriage in mind when he penned Ephesians 6:7–8: 'Serve wholeheartedly, as if you were serving the Lord, not men, because you know that the Lord will reward everyone for whatever good he does . . . (NIV)."

___ d. "In marriage, everything you do counts, even if your spouse ignores you!"

This is what the Rewarded Cycle is all about:

HIS LOVE BLESSES REGARDLESS OF HER RESPECT;

HER RESPECT BLESSES REGARDLESS OF HIS LOVE."

Write your thoughts here regarding the statement you chose. Does the Rewarded Cycle sound too hard? Or is it strangely encouraging, even inspiring?

As a couple you may have had trouble putting the Energizing Cycle in gear. Go over the four statements above that describe how the Rewarded Cycle works. Does the Rewarded Cycle sound helpful or too hard? If you can talk with your spouse about these things, share your deepest thoughts and feelings. (Couples on the Energizing Cycle: read together the third paragraph on book page 272, beginning with "All couples must take heed . . . ." Then talk about how you can keep your marriage on a foundation of rock, never letting it shift to sand.)

3 Read "Heaven's Reward—The Eternal 'Ahhh!'" (book pages 272–74). Have you ever thought of heaven in the terms that Emerson describes in this section? Suppose you could put all the happy, joyful experiences you have ever had into one big package that you could enjoy all the time. When you share your Master's happiness, the intensity of being with Christ forever will be "a trillion times greater" than that! Emerson concludes this section by saying, "When you make a decision to love or respect your spouse, the dividends are without end. Jesus is offering you a bargain. Do a few things on earth in this life and get many things forever in heaven." As you think about hanging in there with a marriage that just doesn't seem to be working, what is

your reaction to Emerson's words? Do you agree that the endless, boundless, indescribable pleasures of heaven will be worth the "momentary affliction" you are feeling now? Write your thoughts here. Be very honest—tell God how it really is. (You can read Emerson's additional comments in *Workbook* Appendix VI.)

If you are able to talk to each other about your marriage, this is a good question to chew on together. Is heaven worth the rough trip you are having here on earth right now? Can you begin to catch a vision of God using your "momentary light affliction" to bring you eternal joy? The first thing the two of you have to do is commit to your marriage because you are doing this as unto Christ, and you look forward to the matchless rewards He has waiting. If you can do that, it will open the way for things to happen here on earth as you struggle between the Crazy Cycle and the Energizing Cycle.

(Couples on the Energizing Cycle: never cease to remind yourselves that you are loving and respecting each other "as unto Christ." When you someday meet Christ face-to-face, He will ask you: "Did you do what you did in your marriage for Me?" How sad if a person must reply, "Lord, I had a good marriage, but I must confess I never thought about You." I know of one wife who had a very good marriage, but she had been overlooking where Christ really fit in. Then she heard the Love and Respect challenge and wrote to say: "The image of myself looking through my husband and seeing Christ was exactly what I needed to hear. Knowing that when I hold my tongue [and] have self-control over my responses, it is not only out of respect for my husband but in obedience to God. What a breakthrough!")

4 Read "What Matters to God, Matters!" (book pages 274–76). Does the "cha-ching!" effect offer any hope and encouragement? Note that Emerson is not talking about earning your salvation; but he is talking about earning rewards (see 1 Corinthians 3:11–15). Which of the following quotes from this section give you hope and encouragement? Pick one and write down why it appeals to you.

____ a. To the world it makes no sense to respect a harsh, unloving husband or to love a contemptuous, disrespectful wife. "But it makes sense to God. These seemingly fruitless efforts matter to God because this is the kind of service He rewards. What is wisdom to God is foolishness to the world" (see 1 Corinthians 3:19; also 1 Peter 2:19; 4:13).

____ b. ". . . look at Ephesians 2:10. We are to do the good works that God has already planned for us. Why? Not to appease the Lord or somehow pay 'just a little bit' for our salvation, but simply to please Him. And when we please Him, He rewards us."

____ c. "Yes, the rewards are waiting. Nothing we do is wasted. The Lord is watching with intense interest. A husband who loves his wife as Christ loved the church, and the wife who respects her husband 'as unto the Lord,' will be rewarded throughout eternity (see Ephesians 5:22–33)."

About rewards, I think:

It may be hard, if not impossible, for the two of you to think about "rewards in heaven" right now. You are having enough struggles on earth. Nonetheless, Scripture does promise rewards for those who earnestly seek to do God's will, however imperfectly. If you have chosen one of the paragraphs above, talk about what it means to you and how its truths can energize you right now. Emerson heard a wife who had been ready to divorce her husband tell a large group of women that the Rewarded Cycle had gotten her eyes off her husband and on the Lord. God revealed to her heart that her first step was to respect her husband unconditionally, "as to the Lord." Until that realization she was feeling defeated and without energy. (Couples on the Energizing Cycle: be sure to look at what Emerson has to say about "not needing rewards, just wanting to reach heaven" [book pages 275–76]. Rewards are important because Jesus reveals them as important. Thank God together for your marriage and any rewards He may have waiting for you.)

5 Read what Emerson says in "It's About You and Jesus Christ" (book pages 276–78). Then answer the three questions below:

a. What is the vital prerequisite if love and respect are to work in your marriage?

b. What is the difference between the successful couple and the unsuccessful one?

c. What is the epitome of immaturity?

The previous three questions are important ones for the struggling couple to answer.

Concerning *a*: if Christ is not the Lord of your life, Love and Respect will not work in God's eyes. Only love and respect done in faith pleases God. If one of you "isn't quite sure" where he or she stands with Christ, this spouse can pray what Emerson suggests: "Lord, I do believe; help my unbelief. I want to follow You, and I want to do this as unto You." (See Mark 9:24.)

Concerning *b*: the difference between the successful couple and the unsuccessful couple is found in Proverbs 24:16. Only Christ can make us righteous, but only we can get up after we fall. Couples who have gotten on the Energizing Cycle have kept dealing with the issues. They never give up!

Concerning *c*: the epitome of immaturity is wanting everything to come easy, with no struggle. Read the letters starting at the bottom of book page 277 to see how two wives took the high road to maturity. (Couples on the Energizing Cycle: read Proverbs 24:16, then talk about why you are successful and what you must continue to do to be successful.)

---

6 Read in "Lord, When Did I Feed You?" (book pages 278–80). What is the basic principle we can take from Christ's parable of the last judgment? Write your answer here:

Do you agree with what Emerson spells out beginning at the bottom of page 279?

". . . ultimately, whatever you do toward your spouse by way of love or respect is not done to motivate your spouse to get off the Crazy Cycle, nor is it to motivate your spouse to meet your needs. Ultimately, you practice love or respect because beyond your spouse you see Jesus Christ and you envision a moment when you will be standing before Him at the final judgment, realizing that your marriage was really a tool and a test to deepen and demonstrate your love and reverence for your Lord."

Write your thoughts here. Tell God what you really feel right now:

 For the struggling couple, the questions above could produce a critical moment. If both of you can agree with what Emerson is saying, you can take a giant step forward in your marriage. If one of you is reluctant or just not sure, the other spouse should be patient and wait for God to work according to His timing. (Couples on the Energizing Cycle: talk about why you show each other love and respect. Is it because you want a happy marriage? Because you are trying to get your spouse to meet your needs? Because you want to serve Christ and reverence Him? All of the above—at least to some degree?)

A Journal of My Journey to Love and Respect

Emerson's Scripture Meditations may serve as a basis for new entries in your journal or you may prefer to record insights and thoughts that have come to you during this session.

Scripture Meditations

1. Scripture acknowledges that we can be afraid, and at least one passage teaches that although we have fears we can deal with them. As Peter told his flock, "Do what is right without being frightened by any fear" (1 Peter 3:6). As a husband, are you afraid of loving your wife, especially if she is disrespectful? Why? As a wife, are you afraid of respecting your husband, especially if he is unloving? Why?

2. "Don't pay back unkind words with unkind words. Instead, pay them back with kind words" (1 Peter 3:9 NIRV). Next time your wife says something disrespectful to you, say something loving; next time your husband says something unloving, say something respectful. Watch what happens. Yes, I've often heard the complaint: "My spouse is different! You don't know my spouse. What you think will happen with my spouse won't happen!" Perhaps not, but why deprive yourself of God's reward by imitating your spouse's negativity? Care enough about God's heart, and what He has in store for you, to do things His way. In all likelihood, the tone of the conflict will turn more positive.

3. "Watch out that you don't lose what you have worked for. Make sure that you get your complete reward" (2 John 1:8 NIRV). The apostle John is teaching something here that has staggering implications. You can go twenty years in your marriage loving and respecting, building up your personal "reward account." Then something could happen in your twenty-first year of marriage and you wind up having contempt, even hatred, for your spouse. John is saying, "Beware, God is gracious; your salvation is assured, but you could fall into sin that would negate some

of the rewards God has planned for you." John is not naïve; he knows believers are being tempted by sin of all kinds, all the time. He is warning his flock because he knew people wouldn't slip into sin when times were good. No, it was far more likely they could lose some of their rewards because they would lose heart in the face of unexpected challenges. John's words are also for you, today, in your marriage. Are you determined to finish faithfully no matter what?

My current thoughts about our marriage:

SESSION FOURTEEN

In preparation for this session, read Chapter Twenty-four, "The Truth Can Make You Free, Indeed" and the Conclusion, "Pink and Blue Can Make God's Purple." The following questions are for an individual or a husband and wife studying together. As in Session 13, the suggestions for spouses studying together are of two kinds: (1) for couples who have slowed the Crazy Cycle, but can't quite get on the Energizing Cycle to their satisfaction; (2) for couples who are on the Energizing Cycle but who can still benefit from what the Rewarded Cycle has to say about how central Jesus Christ should be in a marriage. Remember to answer all unmarked questions first, then answer questions marked by the male or female icon (whichever applies to you). Finally, answer the questions with the couple icon, if you're studying with your mate. (Suggestions for anyone planning to use this study with a small group can be found in *Workbook* Appendix I, page 201.)

Questions for Chapter Twenty-Four

1 Read "Heaven Will Wait—What About Now?" (book pages 281–83). On page 283 Emerson shares his boyhood experiences, when he watched how his mother handled his father's fits of rage. What did she do as she lived with a less-than-perfect spouse? How many things can you learn from her? Write some of them here:

If the two of you are struggling but can still talk together, rejoice in that fact as you begin this session. Compare notes on what you found in the example Emerson's mother set for him as she coped with his father's anger. How easy is it to fall into a "victim mindset"? How hard is it to "choose to be positive"? Do either one of you see yourself having a victim mindset? Are you willing to confess it and move on by making the choice to be positive? (Couples on the Energizing Cycle: you will find much in this session about how to stay there and keep the Crazy Cycle in its cage. Talk together about what it might mean for the two of you to look for "creative alternatives" when you do have a conflict from time to time.)

⌒

2 In "'Sometimes the Issue Is Me!'" (book pages 283–85), Emerson states the Rewarded Cycle Principle (which he admits is useful for anyone on the Energizing Cycle as well). That principle is: no matter how depressing or irritating my spouse might be, my response is my responsibility. What if you are doing everything you can to love or respect your spouse and you still get back cruelty, harshness, contempt, unreasonableness, or indifference? Read the letter from a husband beginning at the bottom of page 284. Then write your thoughts about the Rewarded Cycle Principle. Are you willing to take responsibility for your response, no matter what?

If at all possible, discuss this question together. Talk about Emerson's admission on book page 284 that "in my own marriage, Sarah doesn't cause me to be the way I am; she reveals the way I am. When my reactions to her are unloving, it reveals that I've still got issues. There is still lack of love in my character and soul, and I have to own up to this." Even though Emerson and Sarah are on the Energizing Cycle, there are always moments when they need wisdom from the Rewarded Cycle. As Emerson puts it: "When we are on the Energizing Cycle, we are also on the Rewarded Cycle, given that we are conscious of loving and respecting each other because we do it as unto Christ. The point is, everyone trying to live out the Love and Respect Connection is on a continuum, trying to become a more loving, respectful spouse. No one is perfect; everyone struggles at some point." Do Emerson's words encourage you in your own situation? (Couples on the Energizing Cycle: realize that, like Emerson, you still have "issues" like everyone else. When you talk together about whatever happens in your marriage, each of you should always say, "My response is my responsibility.")

3 Read "What's Inside Will Come Out" and "Inner Freedom Develops Greater Maturity" (book pages 285–87). The grain of sand illustration on page 285 teaches that when your spouse puts heat or pressure on you, you always face a choice (fill in the blanks): "to react in a _____ way or in a _____ way." The "secret" to reacting in a godly way is found in John 8:30–36. In an exchange with Jewish leaders, Jesus reveals the way to true spiritual freedom. What do His words have to do with your marriage? See page 287 for answers and then put some of these truths in your own words here:

 If you are struggling as a couple, the key to ending (or starting to end) your struggles is in the lengthy paragraph at the top of page 287. Read this paragraph together, down through the principle it entails: I can experience hurt, but it is my choice to hate. What is all this saying to each of you? To both of you? (Couples on the Energizing Cycle: you can find much in this section to talk about and digest. Share especially how John 8:36 can keep you on the Energizing Cycle: "So if the Son makes you free, you will be free indeed.")

4 Under "You Can Be Free in Any Circumstance," Emerson continues to describe how you can have inner freedom no matter what situation you are facing. Read 1 Peter 2:16–17. Also, be sure to study Endnote 1 for Chapter Twenty-four, book page 324. Where are you right now with putting Peter's instructions into practice in your marriage?

    ___ a. "Not sure I can do it. You don't know what my spouse is like!"

    ___ b. "I'm willing to try, but I feel so weak and unsure of what to do."

    ___ c. "Through God's grace I will do this; I am trying to do it already!"

    ___ d. I think:

If you and your mate are on the Rewarded Cycle, or trying to be, your answers probably ranged between *b* and *c* above, or perhaps you had your own way of putting it. Look together at the letters on page 289. How did these wives conquer their contempt and lack of respect for their husbands? Also discuss the top paragraph, page 290, in which a husband writes, "It was freeing to reflect on the fact that she was well-intentioned and good-hearted toward me." As Emerson points out, if you believe at all that your spouse is "good-willed" despite those times of being unloving or disrespectful, it can put you on the road to the Rewarded Cycle, and you can build on that. (Couples on the Energizing Cycle: talk about how Peter's instructions in 1 Peter 2:16–17 can apply to your marriage. Are you living as "free men" while you work on your Love and Respect Connection? Look together at End-note 1, Chapter Twenty-four, page 324. Do you agree that ". . . the greatest evidence of submission is Love and Respect"?)

────────

5 Read "Inner Freedom Rewards You with a Legacy" (book pages 290–93). Which of these quotes from this section speak to you the most?

___ a. "Parents want their children to love and respect them, but if they aren't showing love and respect to each other, what kind of legacy are they leaving behind?"

___ b. "Each day you are on the edge of something; you face some kind of crossroads. Today could be the day something happens that will make all the difference. . . . As your children see you living out Christ's words, 'The truth shall make you free,' you will set them on the path of following Jesus as well."

___ c. "You're thinking about mistakes you've made, the times you haven't been a good example, and those numerous scenes where you didn't show love or respect to your spouse. Don't despair. God has a unique way of eliminating past mistakes. Where there has been sin, His grace abounds. He erases your mistakes and puts grace in their place."

My thoughts about leaving a legacy:

If you can discuss this kind of question together, be sure to do so. How does thinking about the legacy you are leaving (how your children see you and how they will respond to Christ) relate to where you are in your marriage? For what happens when love and respect are tried, see the letters on book pages 291–93. (Couples on the Energizing Cycle: you will want to think about the legacy you are leaving. Have you even thought of how your Love and Respect Connection looks to your children? What specifically can you do, or continue to do, when your kids are watching that which will prepare them for having their own families some day?)

—————————

6 "The Reward of Winning Your Spouse God's Way" (book pages 293–96) includes several letters from husbands and wives who are moving forward on the Rewarded Cycle by living out Love and Respect. Which of the following excerpts contain kernels of truth you can use right now?

_____ a. "I wanted her to respect me and be my friend—neither of which I was experiencing . . . . Thanks be to God for knowledge that leads to understanding and allows me to act lovingly in service to Jesus Christ."

_____ b. "I changed my attitude. I changed my tone of voice and my facial expressions. I even changed my prayers from 'bless me and change him' to 'change me and bless him.'"

_____ c. "My situation is not any easier at home, my husband has been 'on the run' from the Lord for many years now, but I do not feel so hopeless and, therefore, do not need to have the final word . . . , worry about a decision, etc. And by honoring my husband . . . I am choosing life, Christ's life, and then I am blessed. Even if my husband never changes, I know the Lord wants me to honor Him."

Most meaningful to me of the quotes on the previous page is _____ because:

As you have seen while studying Sessions 13 and 14, the Rewarded Cycle is for couples in many different states of mind. They know love and respect is the way, but walking in that way is a struggle. If the two of you have been able to discuss any of the questions in these sessions, thank God for a major step of progress. If one or more of the quotes above speak to you, talk about why and what it might mean to your marriage. (Couples on the Energizing Cycle: you may complete this final session in the Rewarded Cycle and have one of two basic reactions: (1) "All of this is nice, but we really didn't need it" or (2) "Now we see what love and respect is really about. It's not about us; first and foremost, it is about our relationship to Jesus Christ. When that is strong, our marriage is strong." Carefully read the paragraphs on the bottom of page 295 and the top of page 296. Do you agree that once a couple attempts the vital step toward marital maturity that the tests will come? How can you be ready?)

Questions for Conclusion

7 Read book pages 297–98. Why did one husband find the Love and Respect Conference to be a "breath of fresh air"? What is the real purpose behind showing each other love and respect? Put your thoughts in writing here.

Do you agree with the husband who wrote in to say that at a Love and Respect Conference he was impressed the most by the Rewarded Cycle? If you have not attended one of these conferences, perhaps it is time to do so. For information on how to attend a Love and Respect Conference, or how to purchase a video of a conference, please go to http://www.loveandrespect.com. (Couples on the Energizing Cycle: set aside time to go over C-O-U-P-L-E and C-H-A-I-R-S and how you can live out these principles by keeping your eyes on your ultimate goal—glorifying God and obeying His Word. During a Love and Respect Conference, Emerson asks each husband and wife in attendance to "see" with the eyes of faith that just beyond the shoulder of his/her spouse stands Jesus Christ. Jesus is saying, "This isn't about your spouse, who may not deserve love or respect. This is about your living with love and respect as you show reverence for Me." With this image in mind, husbands and wives can go through C-O-U-P-L-E and C-H-A-I-R-S and receive divine help for living out any of these principles. A husband may not want to say, "I'm sorry," but he makes peace with his wife anyway, because just over her shoulder he sees his divine Master, and he does what he needs to do as unto Christ. A wife may rebel against acknowledging her husband's authority, but she does so anyway, because just over his shoulder she sees the Lord, and she does what she needs to do as unto Him. Living out C-O-U-P-L-E and C-H-A-I-R-S "as unto Christ" does not prohibit disagreeing with each other and confronting issues; the couple living on the Energizing Cycle "as unto Christ" can deal with any problem. They look at each other, and just over each spouse's shoulder is Jesus Christ. This is not just "incentive to be good"; it is power to live with love and respect.)

————————

8 On book page 299 Emerson relates how "two can become one" as stated in Ephesians 5:31–33: ". . . as a husband puts on love, especially during conflict, his wife will feel one with him. When a wife puts on respect during those moments, the husband will feel one with his wife. A disagreement may not be solved, but oneness will be experienced. When a wife feels her need for love is met, she bonds with her husband. When a husband feels his need for respect is being met, he bonds with his wife. This can happen simultaneously. Two do, indeed, become one!" Do you think what Emerson says is possible for you and your spouse? What stands in the way?

Before writing your thoughts, consider these additional ideas by Emerson:

"In order to be 'one' as God intended, the Bible teaches we need to depend on Christ. Do you find encouragement in these words spoken by Christ: 'Apart from Me you can do nothing' (John 15:5)? As a man do you feel it is 'unmanly' to depend on Christ? Can you show love to your disrespectful wife in your own natural strength? As a wife, you can love naturally (it is the way God created you), but you don't respect naturally when you feel unloved. As a man, or as a woman, do you admit you need Christ's help to show your spouse love or respect? What a comfort to know God has sent 'the Helper,' His Holy Spirit, to help the one who looks to Him! Does knowing God is there to help you uplift your heart?" Write your thoughts:

Like so many questions in these sessions covering the Rewarded Cycle, this may be difficult for you and your mate to discuss. But if you can talk about it at all, rejoice in your progress! Talk about your conflicts and disagreements. Why do these differences of opinion leave you feeling your needs are not being met—hers for love, his for respect? What would happen if you had a disagreement, agreed to disagree, and assured each other of your mutual love and respect? Be sure to look at the last paragraph of this section starting on the bottom line of book page 299. The best kind of help is available for the asking. (Couples on the Energizing Cycle: you can benefit from evaluating how well you "agree to disagree." During times of conflict or disagreement, does she still feel loved? Does he still feel respected? How can you both be sure of this? [For ideas, review *Love & Respect* Appendix A, "A Lexicon of Love and Respect . . . ," especially pages 305–6. Also see *Love & Respect* Appendix C, "How to Ask Your Mate to Meet Your Needs."])

9 In "Have You Really Tried Prayer?" (book pages 300–3), Emerson uses another analogy to describe being one in Christ. When pink (the wife) blends with blue (the husband) the result is purple (God's color of royalty). The challenge is in the blending. The answer to "how to blend" is in the verse that began this book: Ephesians 5:33. Write that verse here, followed by your statement of commitment to pray— really pray—for the power to allow God to fulfill His desires in you.

If one or both of you is still struggling, blending your pink and blue to make God's purple may sound too difficult. But do not put the idea totally out of reach, because it may be only a prayer away. Read the letters on book pages 301–2. Then consider the Prayer of Commitment on page 302. If you can pray this prayer, do it now. (Couples on the Energizing Cycle: you will also want to go over the Prayer of Commitment. It may be of benefit to write out this prayer, inserting your own thoughts and decisions as you go.)

A JOURNAL OF MY JOURNEY TO LOVE AND RESPECT

Since this is the final session in your study of Love and Respect, you may want to look back to where you were when you started and record your thoughts about the progress you have made.

SCRIPTURE MEDITATIONS

1. "For from within, out of the heart . . . proceed . . . envy, slander, pride and foolishness" (Mark 7:21–22). What is Jesus saying to each one of us? That our response is always our responsibility! Our Lord does not let us rationalize our sins. When we do wrong, it is a choice of the heart, who we are deep within. There is no copping out, no blaming others. The husband who barks, "I was unloving because I get no respect" only confirms Christ's words. The wife who shrills, "I can't respect him; I get no love!" speaks from a heart that needs Christ's touch. Pray daily for His touch, and always begin, "Lord, help me. My response is my responsibility."

2. Paul told Timothy, "Set an example . . . in speech, in life, in love, in faith and in purity" (1 Timothy 4:12 NIV). We all know the overwhelming power of example, especially in the home in front of the children. When we come across as unloving, angry, disrespectful, or harsh, it drowns out all our advice, teaching, instruction, or admonition. When one of our personal needs goes unmet and we lash out with hate or contempt, the kids only learn that our faith in Christ appears meaningless. If you have already blown it, ask God for His abundant grace and forgiveness. If you are

blowing it right now, with children still in the home who are watching you, ask God for help—the power to love, the strength to respect. He will grant what you need, as you trust in Him.

3. It is right and good for a husband to love his wife and for a wife to respect her husband. But a husband will suffer when loving a disrespectful wife, and a wife will suffer when respecting an unloving husband. What incentive is there, then, to suffer like this? Peter tell us: ". . . when you do what is right and suffer for it . . . this finds favor with God" (1 Peter 2:20). Yes, as you endure the suffering your spouse may be causing you, it wins God's favor. This is something of which the carnal world knows nothing. The unbeliever sneers, "You are stupid for suffering this way. Be done with this!" But the believer knows that the day is coming when those who suffer this way will be seen as wise, not stupid, because the favor of God rests on them. Be encouraged. You have God's Word on it!

> Now may the God and Father of our Lord Jesus Christ,
> by the power of the Holy Spirit, bless you with wisdom
> and strength to grace your marriage with love and respect.
> And may He eternally reward you because you chose
> to trust and obey Him. Amen.

My final thoughts as I conclude my study of *Love and Respect*:

APPENDIX I

Suggestions for Group Leaders

USING THE *LOVE & RESPECT* *WORKBOOK* IN A GROUP SETTING

Before using this workbook with your small group . . .

1. Read the introductory pages, read the introductory pages, "Before You Start Your Study of *Love & Respect*" (page 6). Become familiar with the workbook's primary purpose: to take an individual spouse or a couple through each chapter of *Love & Respect* as they interact with the thinking of its author. Dr. Emerson Eggerichs, in addition to seminary degrees, has an M.A. in Communication and a Ph.D. in Child and Family Ecology. Beyond that, he spent more than twenty-five years in the pastorate, where he counseled many couples struggling in their marriages. In 1998, as a result of meditating on Ephesians 5:33, he experienced a significant breakthrough in his understanding of this marital struggle. At that time, he recognized why this struggle happened between good-willed people. Emerson felt that God illumined his heart, so to speak, to see the remedy to these marital tensions. The *Love & Respect* message is this remedy. In 1999 Emerson left a thriving congregation of 2,000 to found Love and Respect Ministries. Since then, he and his wife, Sarah, have conducted Love and Respect Conferences in churches and other settings throughout the nation.

2. Complete several sessions of the workbook to become thoroughly acquainted with its design and function. You should always be a session or two ahead of the group to provide adequate time to internalize the material and decide which questions to emphasize with your group. If possible, have your spouse study along with you and use the discussion ideas for couples throughout the workbook. (Look for the icon that indicates questions for spouses studying together.)

Additional helpful information for the group leader is contained in Appendices II–VI (see pages 205–223). All of these additional resources are a gold mine of information for a group leader. Read and study them, then use what works for your group.

3. Check your leadership style. Facilitating a group study of a book like *Love & Respect* is a great responsibility. The spouses in your group represent marriages in different circumstances and stages—some strong, others weak. As you lead your group, seek to be:

Relaxed and casual, but organized and able to keep things moving. Let people share, give opinions, and even disagree a bit, but don't be afraid to sum things up and move to the next question or topic.

Caring and sensitive, always trying to be aware of what others might be thinking or feeling at the moment. Some couples in your group will probably see a lot of humor in certain questions and be quite able to enjoy what is going on. Others could be hurting and unhappy, not finding the proceedings to be as much fun. You may spot couples or perhaps individuals you need to contact outside the group, to guide them in their study, pray with them, or possibly refer them to someone who can give help that you cannot.

Acceptant and nonthreatening. For example, if someone comes up with an opinion that is totally counter to what Emerson sometimes refers to as "typical" or "generally speaking," do not be defensive or argumentative. Let everyone who wishes to give opinions, then sum up by saying, "According to Emerson's extensive experience and research, this is what he finds to be the norm or what is typical of men and women, husbands and wives. He knows there are exceptions to any 'general rule,' but he has also found that regardless of how people think or act, they all need love and respect."

Experienced and empathetic. Ideally, you and your spouse have studied the workbook together, and you have learned how to slow and stop the Crazy Cycle. You know what it takes to keep the Energizing Cycle humming. And you know and readily admit that at times you need wisdom and humility that you can get only from the Rewarded Cycle. Your enthusiasm and transparency about sharing your own problems and what you and your spouse have learned will do much to get the rest of the group to relax and open up to what *Love & Respect* has to offer. (You don't have to have a perfect marriage to qualify to lead a small group through the workbook. Ideally, however, if you and your spouse are leading the group together, it would be beneficial for you to have worked completely through the workbook and be in agreement about living in the Rewarded Cycle in your own marriage.)

Willing to use tough love in regard to everyone doing the homework. As a rule, any couple willing to join a study of *Love & Respect* should be highly motivated to put in the necessary time to improve their marriage. If you are holding meetings once a week, suggest that couples will need to invest a minimum of two hours weekly to the workbook. As they get into their study, they may soon be spending much more than that. Remind everyone: "Your study of *Love & Respect* should be top priority because your marriage is top priority. Your *Love & Respect Workbook* assignments are 'homework' done for the sake of your marriage and your home. This study has to do with improving (even saving) your marriage. It deserves your best effort because your marriage deserves your best effort."

Dependent on God's leading. Prayer must be a major part of your preparation for every meeting. And while leading a meeting, be praying silently: "Lord, help us all right now; give me the right words to say, or prompt another member of our group to share something that can help someone else."

If you get a question you can't answer, admit it and say you will try to find an answer by next meeting. Throughout the week, pray for each of your group members, and for each marriage represented. Contact your group members during the week to see how they are doing. If a couple is on the Crazy Cycle, offer to pray with them over the phone. Never be pushy, but always be available and interested.

4. Plan your meetings and what you want to cover. As you have probably already seen, there is a lot of material in this workbook. The fourteen sessions are organized around the flow of material in *Love & Respect*, as you move from the Crazy Cycle to the Energizing Cycle and finally the Rewarded Cycle. Some sessions cover one chapter of *Love & Respect*; others cover two chapters, and a few cover three. Obviously many sessions contain far more material than you can cover in one meeting. You will want to pick and choose questions that you believe will meet the needs of your group.

Also important is how much time you have for each meeting. You should plan on one hour minimum, but ninety minutes or two hours would be better, particularly as people get involved in discussing their problems and sharing insights they have gleaned from reading *Love & Respect*. As you divide the material to develop meeting plans, keep these points in mind:

a. Go through a session and decide how much of it you will use for a meeting.

b. Choose questions that cover the key truths of a given chapter in *Love & Respect*. All of the material is interesting but keep in mind your goal for the meeting—the essential points you want to make.

c. Go over all the questions you think you might use and analyze each one for how suitable it is for "public group consumption." Some of the questions asked in this workbook are sensitive; the answers people write will be, in some cases, things they want to keep private. Some questions are probably best avoided altogether; others could be used if you do some checking with your group members and also give some introductory explanations. Always stress that no one has to talk or share what is written in his or her workbook.

d. For more help planning meetings, see http://loveandrespect.com/LEADER/ and view "Meeting Plans for Your Small Group," which gives ideas for planning fourteen meetings that cover the fourteen sessions in the workbook. They can easily be expanded to cover more meetings, according to the interests of your group.

Appendix II

1 PETER 3:2: ADDRESSED TO GOD OR TO WIVES?

I am sometimes asked about my emphasis on 1 Peter 3:2 and why I take the position that the Greek word *phobos* should be translated "respectful behavior" toward husbands, which is the way the New American Standard Bible translates it.

Those who challenge my preference for the NASB translation refer to the New International Version of 1 Peter 3:2, which translates *phobos* as "reverence of your lives." This translation implies that wives are not commanded to show respectful behavior toward their husbands; instead their respect, or reverence, is to be given to God. My reply is that a wife who reverences God will come across in respectful ways to her husband. First Peter 3:2 is part of a larger passage—1 Peter 2:12–3:7—within which context it is clear why the NASB translates 1 Peter 3:2 as it does.

Peter's theme throughout 1 Peter 2:12–3:7 is that Christians are first to have vertical respect (or reverence) toward God, and then live out their reverence for Him with horizontal respect toward others. As Peter puts it, because of our vertical relationship to God we are to show "excellent behavior," specifically submissive behavior that comes across to others as honorable and respectful. For example:

In 2:12, why are we to show excellent behavior among the Gentiles (unbelievers)? Because it will glorify God.

In 2:13, why are we to submit to human institutions and authority? For the Lord's sake.

In 2:15, why are we to do what is right before other people? It is God's will.

In 2:16, since we are free, why should we be sure never to use that freedom as a cover for evil? Because we are God's bondslaves.

In 2:17, when we are commanded to honor all, love the brotherhood, and honor the king, we realize this means unconditional love and honor. Those we are commanded to honor and love may not deserve such treatment.

In 2:18, why are servants to submit by showing respect toward those who are harsh and unreasonable, not just toward those who are gentle and good? Because this finds God's favor.

In 2:19, why should a believer do what is right toward people? Because this is how to follow Christ's example.

Regarding wives, what is Peter's application of his concept of living with excellence? Go to 1 Peter 3:1, which begins, "In the same way, you wives be submissive to your own husbands . . . ." In the same way as what? In the same way Christians are to be submissive to (have respect for) those already mentioned in the total passage: kings, governors, other believers, masters (review 1 Peter 2:13–18). In 3:1–2 why are wives to act in this same submissive way in order to win their disobedient husbands? Because their actions and attitudes are precious to God.

So, coming back to the original question, does 1 Peter 3:2 say a wife wins her disobedient husband through her respectful behavior (NASB translation) or through her reverence for God (NIV translation)? As I like to say with questions like this: Yes! These choices are the front and back of the same coin. When a believing wife reverences God, her behavior spills over onto her husband as respect. On the other side of the coin, when she shows respectful behavior toward her husband, it comes out of her reverence for God, her "excellent behavior," which is what Peter has been talking about throughout the last half of 1 Peter chapter two!

The overall tone and message of 1 Peter 2:12–3:7 teaches us to show excellent behavior and a reverence for God, which displays itself through submissiveness that comes across as unconditional respect.

APPENDIX III

FORGIVENESS HAS TWO LEVELS

When counseling a couple on the Crazy Cycle, I find it helps many spouses to understand that forgiveness involves two levels:

1. Forgiving a person for having a personal preference at odds with your own personal preference.

2. Forgiving a person for a moral transgression.

First, how should you forgive someone for "wronging" you by preferring something you do not? Consider some examples:

- A husband prefers to leave the sink or a room (or the entire house!) less than neat, but his wife prefers everything neat and clean.

- A wife prefers to drive the car on a full tank or nearly so, but the husband prefers to live on the edge and drive it another twenty miles with the red "Fuel Low" indicator blinking merrily.

- A husband prefers to save "discretionary money" but his wife prefers to spend it.

All of the above examples are personal preferences, not moral transgressions. But the "rub" comes when one spouse starts resenting the other spouse for having different personal preferences. Then the personal preference can become a supposed moral transgression. The "logic" runs thusly: "If I mattered to you, you would do it my way. I can see, however, that you don't care. Obviously, I don't matter!" Easily carried a bit further, this kind of logic continues: "Because you don't care and think I don't matter, you are wrong, unloving, disrespectful—even ungodly!"

Actually, the only thing "ungodly" that is going on is that you have made a moral mountain out of a personal preference molehill. God knew that Christians, especially spouses, would experience tension over personal preferences, and He inspired writers such as the apostle Paul to lay down helpful principles about how to handle this kind of thing (see, for example, Romans 14). If you ignore God's principles and become bitter and unforgiving over personal preference problems, it reveals a character flaw in you, not your spouse. Because your husband has his own standard of cleanliness (that is, being comfortable with less-than-perfect neatness) does not mean he is ungodly. Because your wife is not as frugal as you are and loves to find a good sale that may blow the budget for that month, she is not a loose woman. To get upset to the point of becoming angry and unforgiving is to be judgmental and self-righteous.

When I am counseling a couple, right about here is where the wife may get a bit exasperated. Her husband is driving her nuts with his sloppiness. Can't he do anything to help just a little? My reply is that having differences on personal preferences leaves plenty of room for disagreement, debate, and even some anger (as long as the anger doesn't last past sundown (see Ephesians 4:26–27). If a couple has truly bought into *Love & Respect* principles and techniques, they can work out any disagreement. Messy husbands can reform (at least to a point) because they want to love their wives better. Spendthrift wives can reform (at least to a point) because they want to respect their husbands more.

But what cannot happen is for one spouse or the other to stay angry and unforgiving over differences in personal preferences. You may become upset by your spouse's choice to act in a certain way (the personal preference), but to stay argumentative and bitter about it is overkill. To repeat: *a personal preference is not a moral transgression.* To take offense at something that is not a true offense flies in the face of all that the Love and Respect Connection stands for in your marriage.

But what about the other level of forgiveness? What about forgiving things that are true offenses because they are moral transgressions? And within the boundaries of marriage, how does one tell the difference between a personal preference and something serious enough to fall in the category of "moral transgression"? I believe this kind of sin is committed consciously and willfully. In the New Testament there is no final summary of such trespasses, but in Galatians 5:19–21 Paul mentions such sins as immorality, idolatry, and drunkenness and ends a rather long list with ". . . and things like these . . . ." Obviously, Paul is intending to be illustrative, not exhaustive. He is talking about following after the flesh (the sinful nature, see Galatians 5:16–17) in such a way that it grieves God's heart and deeply wounds your spouse.

If you are the spouse who is wounded, how do you respond to "things like these"? First of all, you must confront such sins in the right spirit. For example, suppose you learn of your mate's act of adultery. You may be stunned, devastated, and extremely angry, but you should not confront your spouse with lasting bitterness and contempt. God forgives a momentary angry response, but a continually bitter person cannot be God's instrument to restore a straying spouse. The confrontation needs to be done with a respectful and forgiving spirit, even if your heart is breaking. A forgiving spirit says, "I refuse to become a bitter and contemptuous soul, though you have wounded me with a near fatal blow."

"But," you may object, "if I display a respectful and forgiving spirit, my spouse will not repent!" The error here is to think that a contemptuous and continually angry spirit is the means God intends to use to motivate a spouse to repent. This is not God's means to achieve His holy end. Your truthful and humble confrontation of sin by stating the clear facts can lead to another's repentance when your belligerence never will.

"Okay," you might respond, "what if my sinful spouse remains unrepentant after being confronted and accuses me of being judgmental and unforgiving?" Unrepentant spouses often make this claim. The typical line is, "You are so intolerant and self-righteous. Don't judge, lest you be judged!" The offender uses this kind of line to shame the godly spouse into the conclusion, "to prove I am forgiving and not judgmental, I will no longer confront my spouse's wrongdoing." The spouse who has been wronged must not fall for this kind of manipulation. Confrontation must still occur, but in a forgiving manner.

Some spouses may question me right here because they know what Jesus says in Luke 17:3: "If your brother sins, rebuke him; and if he repents, forgive him." What if your spouse refuses to repent? Is Jesus saying that you don't have to forgive as long as your spouse remains unrepentant? That's a fair question. My answer is that the kind of forgiveness Jesus mentions in Luke 17:3 (the ending of the confrontation or rebuke) is different from the spirit of forgiveness, which Jesus also teaches in many places (see for example, Matthew 18:21–35). A spouse who has been wronged can forgive the offending spouse (with a spirit of forgiveness from the heart), but still confront the offender until he or she repents. Having a forgiving spirit does not mean that you announce, "Because I have a forgiving spirit, I will no longer confront your adultery and alcoholism. Go ahead and continue in your sin." Jesus would not want you to be so foolish or uncaring. He intends that you care enough to confront, but in a loving and respectful way.

For example, a husband can have a forgiving spirit toward his wife for her alcoholism, but for her sake there must be confrontation and consequences. Having a forgiving spirit does not mean letting the transgressor off the hook. The wife may adamantly insist she has changed (alcoholics often do), but somehow she turns up drunk again. The husband must say, "Honey, I love you and I forgive you, but I cannot trust you."

It is important to differentiate between forgiving and trusting. To be real, repentance must lead to some kind of change in behavior or attitude. Paul taught his listeners to "repent and turn to God, performing deeds appropriate to repentance" (Acts 26:20). Some evidence should exist that the sinner has sincerely turned the corner on his or her sin. When this "fruit" is plainly there, the offended party should be encouraged and thank God. Yes, the fear that "it could happen again" may always be there, but it should not be allowed to control the situation. If an offending spouse repents and has a real change in behavior, full forgiveness should be extended. You should not be in your spouse's face confronting a grievous sin that is no longer there. You stop dwelling on the past and look to the future.

Sadly, a spouse may commit grievous sins, but after supposedly "forgiving" those sins the offended party ends up committing worse sins. I have watched this kind of thing happen all too often over the years. The sinful spouse comes clean in repentant humility, but the offended spouse chooses to be relentless with questioning and accusing. For example, a husband commits adultery and then repents, asking God's forgiveness and his wife's. His fellowship with God is restored, but his wife is bitter and judgmental. Even though the husband turns his heart back to Christ and tries in every way he can to restore the marriage, his wife continues to defame him to anyone who will listen, including their children.

What is more common than the repentant spouse who remains unforgiven is the spouse who refuses to repent, or the spouse who claims repentance but the "appropriate deeds" don't follow. Returning to the example of the alcoholic wife, her husband can have a forgiving spirit, but that does not include allowing her to go to a bar or to stay home alone for any period of time. The facts are clear: at present, her addiction does not make her trustworthy regarding alcohol. The husband should say, "I love you, but you must go to the rehab center at the hospital. You are too weak to fight your addiction alone."

There is no contradiction between extending forgiveness and enacting consequences for the offender. Because you forgive someone doesn't mean that everything goes on just as it did before, that nothing has to change. For example, a wife may forgive her husband's adultery with his secretary, but that does not mean the husband can continue to work with the secretary. The forgiving wife need not "prove" her forgiveness by allowing her husband to do whatever he chooses in relationship to the secretary. But the husband does need to prove that he is truly repentant and intends to be loyal to his wife by "bear[ing] fruit in keeping with repentance" (see Matthew 3:1–10).

I know of one man who committed adultery with a female associate at work, and he decided his only course of action was to resign. He did this not only to remove further temptation, but also to demonstrate to his wife that his repentance was real. He knew her forgiveness was real, but he also knew he had to reestablish trust. The onus was on him, not his wife. This marriage has been restored now for over fifteen years. When the husband quit his job he took a huge hit financially, but God honored his decision. Today, he owns his own company and loves what he is doing. He and his wife love each other more than ever and are actively involved together in ministries at their local church.

But what about the wife who confronts her husband's sin and he refuses to repent? In 1 Peter 3:1–2 the wife is called upon to win her disobedient husband "without a word." Peter understood that after awhile a wife's words of rebuke repulse a disobedient husband. Her fire and brimstone preaching just turns him off. From a human perspective, "without a word" makes no sense, especially to a wife who is continually being wronged. However, God's revelation is to be obeyed. When it is clear that her husband will not listen, she must cease her confrontation. She must walk in a quiet, gentle, respectful, and forgiving spirit, trusting that God will defend her and convict her husband.

Does Scripture teach that a wife should go quietly on and on while her unrepentant husband continues, for example, to commit adultery? If the transgressing party refuses to repent and cut off the adulterous relationship, divorce may be inevitable (see Matthew 5:32; 19:9). The innocent spouse may have a forgiving spirit, but ongoing hardness of heart, unfaithfulness, and betrayal by the guilty spouse can kill whatever is left of the marriage.

What about physical abuse? The abused spouse can have a forgiving spirit, but immediate physical separation may be necessary. An abused wife need not "prove her forgiveness" by subjecting herself and her children to more violence. That would not only be absurd, it could be fatal. My counsel is that an abused wife should bodily remove herself and her children from a violent husband. There are people in every community ready and able to help abused wives.

I do not know your situation. Every marriage, every family, is different. But I do have a strong conviction. In any Bible-believing church there should be at least one person who can counsel you with godly wisdom. Paul says as much when he writes, "Is it possible that there is nobody among you wise enough to judge a dispute between believers?" (1 Corinthians 6:5 NIV). God is saying that there is such a person and that you must seek that person out and ask for help. For the sake of your children, for your own sake and for God's honor, find that person! God will direct your steps. I have seen it happen.

Do not assume that the only person who can help you is the pastor. It may well be that your pastor or an elder could be this person, but there may be others. Every church I have ever visited has a handful of happily married compassionate people who are humble servants ready to respond to a person in deep crisis. The ground rule is simple: when you turn to this person or couple for assistance, your attitude must not be, "I want to tell you the evils my spouse has committed against me to destroy me." Instead, your attitude is to be, "My spouse has stumbled and sinned. I need God's wisdom to restore our marriage. I want to face my own sin, which has contributed to this problem, but I also want to confront my spouse's sin in the right spirit. Will you help me?"

One last word: Jesus instructs us to do this. Humanly, there may be no reason to believe a sinful, straying spouse will respond to confrontation. I have seen, however, that when God's word is obeyed, it brings God's convicting power. When you step out in faith and in the spirit of forgiveness, love, and respect, God shows up. One person who had been confronted by his spouse and me said, "You have restored my confidence in the church." This carnal Christian knew what was happening and was thankful that people cared enough to get involved.

In another situation the person who was confronted told me, "After the confrontation, I lived in fear that God would take my life." I never advise telling someone, "You better shape up or God will get you." Nonetheless, loving but firm confrontation can bring people under deep conviction! The confronted person may act indifferent or rebellious, but things can be happening in his or her soul. I cannot count the number of small groups who confronted a wayward member of their Bible study for wrong behavior and that person returned to the fold. This works more often than most want to believe. And the reason it works is because God tells us to do it, and He backs up His commands.

APPENDIX IV

DOES EPHESIANS 5:21 SAY WIVES DON'T
HAVE TO SUBMIT TO HUSBANDS?

Contrary to what some teachers and leaders in the church espouse, Ephesians 5:21—"Submit to one another out of reverence for Christ" (NIV)—does not "cancel out" Ephesians 5:22, where wives are instructed to "submit to your husbands as to the Lord" (NIV). In Chapter Seventeen of *Love & Respect*, I pointed out that the Greek word translated "submit" is *hupotasso*. Literally, this is a compound word meaning to rank under or place under. In Ephesians 5:23–24, Paul explains why a wife is to "rank under" or "place herself under" her husband: "For the husband is the head of the wife as Christ is the head of the church. . . . Now as the church submits to Christ, so also wives should submit to their husbands in everything" (NIV). Paul is simply saying that as Christ has authority over the church, so the husband has authority over his wife. But most importantly, the husband's authority is to be motivated by love and is based on his responsibility to be a Christ-figure. As Christ loved the church and gave Himself up for her, the husband is to be willing to die for his wife if necessary (see Ephesians 5:25–29).

Because God has given the husband primary responsibility, He has also given him primary authority. Nowhere in Ephesians 5 is the wife called to be the head of her husband. Nor is the wife called upon to be the Christ-figure dying for her husband. This kind of "mutuality" does not exist in the text. In summary, any teaching on "mutual submission" should never negate the fact that Scripture clearly and ultimately calls the wife to defer to her husband's God-given authority and responsibility. If a wife protests, saying, "We are equal; we are to submit equally to one another," she will hurt and frustrate her husband. Few things are as demeaning and disrespectful to a husband as denying or ignoring his primary responsibility before God. Those who seek to be politically correct might scoff, "Who cares how a man feels? He needs to get over it!" A wise wife, however, not only cares about how her good-willed husband feels, she understands this is how God created him, and she seeks to help him with his awesome task of leading and protecting her. Thus, she places herself under his authority and enjoys his protection.

Having said all this, we must note that while the husband has the greater general authority, his wife is not without specific authority in at least two areas. First, Scripture teaches that the husband is to submit to his wife's sexual authority. In 1 Corinthians 7:4, Paul writes, "The wife does not have authority over her own body, but the husband does; and likewise also the husband does not have authority over his own body, but the wife does." Half the time, so to speak, in the sexual realm (and this is a colossal realm!) the wife has authority over her husband's body. At those times the husband must submit to his wife's God-given authority, right, or need. For example, for a change she may need him sexually, and he should submit to her request to be sexually intimate. Or, she may be exhausted from a horrific day caring for sick kids and prefers to abstain from sex, at least that night. The loving husband must submit to his wife's request.

But doesn't 1 Corinthians 7:4 also say the husband has authority over his wife in the sexual realm? Clearly, it does, so how can this be worked out if both spouses have equal authority over the other's body? I believe Scripture is calling both spouses to mutually submit to the other's authority and need! Because both have equal authority, both must mutually submit. Is this a mystical idea that is impossible to apply? A simple explanation is to strike a balance (find a happy medium). An important point to grasp about mutual sexual submission is that it does not always have to be simultaneous. Work out a way you can "give preference to one another in honor" (Romans 12:10). The couple practicing Love and Respect can agree on a sexual pattern that is mutually acceptable to both of them. Paul leaves each couple to work out 1 Corinthians 7:4 in their own way, doing so with the confidence that God will guide both spouses in this area of mutual submission.

Does this mean there won't be times of tension or disagreement when an agreed upon pattern doesn't work out? No—but a good thing to keep in mind is that in Ephesians 5:21 Paul instructs husbands and wives to submit to each other *"out of reverence for Christ"* (NIV, italics mine). You aren't playing some kind of game of marital *quid pro quo.* You are using your marriage as a practical laboratory for living out your reverence for Christ. In the midst of the tension there is always a Third Party who can be trusted to give you help. Because you try to reverence Christ, He is there to get you through the tough times.

For example, I once counseled a husband who felt he was being deprived sexually. His wife seemed repulsed by the idea of having sex on a regular basis, and this had become a huge problem for them. I advised him to trust and reverence the Lord in the midst of his frustration and to seek to consistently love his wife as a person, even if she didn't always respond sexually. It is amazing what prayer and love can do! Their sexual intimacy is now better than ever. The husband, a medical doctor, truly sees God's hand in what has happened. You can too, if you reverence Him when you are feeling disrespected or unloved.

A second way a husband submits is indirectly stated in Ephesians 5:33, the passage on which *Love & Respect* is based: ". . . each one of you also must love his wife as he loves himself, and the wife must respect her husband" (NIV). I have learned in my marriage to Sarah that loving her isn't always convenient or easy, especially when I feel disrespected. So, in order to love Sarah at such times, I must choose to submit to Sarah's need to be loved. In that way, I show my submission to God's command and my reverence for Christ. And in the same way, respecting me isn't always easy for Sarah, especially when she feels unloved! In order to respect me at such times, she must choose to submit to my need to be respected. When she shows me respect, she shows her submission to God's command and her reverence for Christ.

Because Paul commands us to be subject to one another in Ephesians 5:21, and then in the immediate context he teaches husbands to love and wives to respect, I believe love and respect are part of mutual submission. I also believe that, outside the bedroom, mutual submission can and should happen simultaneously. In all other situations in marriage, we can simultaneously submit to each other's need to feel loved or respected. For example, during a serious disagreement Sarah and I can mutually submit by giving each other love or respect even though we remain at loggerheads about the decision over, let's say, buying a security system for our home versus increasing our health insurance. She wants the system; I want the insurance. When I truly seek to meet Sarah's need to feel loved, even while we are arguing in favor of our own position, the "conflict" does not escalate to hostility. In this case, even though I defer 90 percent of the time to what my wife wants for our home, I feel I have to go with the health insurance, where our coverage is dangerously low at some points. But in making my decision I am still called to submit to Sarah's need to feel loved; I don't have to be hateful as I make my choice. By the same token, Sarah does not close off her spirit. She respects my decision and me, even though she is disappointed. (It turns out that a few months later we were able to buy the security system anyway, so we were both happy.)

Admittedly, I have used a situation where everything came out nicely in the end. You may be saying, "That's fine for you, Emerson, but with my husband and me, I would want the security system and he would want a new set of golf clubs. According to your thinking, he gets his clubs and we get no security system, even though crime is going up in our town every month. I have to live with his bad decision, and that is just not right." My answer is that I have counseled many wives who have had to live with bad decisions by their husbands. In fact, Sarah has had to live with a number of mine. I am not saying that submitting to a bad decision is easy, but in the long run it will pay off. I have seen many wives override their husbands again and again with a disrespectful attitude. Finally the continual disrespect gets to these husbands. They say to their wives, "Fine, you take over; have it your way"—and they retreat into being uninvolved and passive. Later, their wives come to me and say they can't understand why their husbands aren't more involved with them on much of anything. There is no connection, no intimacy—he is just "out of it."

My point is that some bad decisions need to go the husband's way. If the wife submits and is quiet (not cold, complaining, or bitter), she has a better platform for making her case next time. What I have seen with thousands of couples is that a good-willed husband seldom ignores his wife's reasoned, respectful appeals on a continual basis. When a wife respectfully and calmly presents her position to her husband, he will seldom take issue with her motherly and womanly desires.

I believe the real issue is not with male dominance and bad decision-making, resulting in harm to wives. Yes, that can happen, but it does not happen that often among good-willed couples. The real issue is with female dominance and passive, angry husbands. What I am trying to get across to wives, and husbands, is that hierarchy and authority are not teachings designed to keep the wife in subjection, treated like a doormat. Instead, if the wife submits respectfully, it motivates the husband to stay engaged in the awesome task of leading his home on all fronts, including being the spiritual leader, which is the deepest longing of the wife. The problem isn't with a husband denying the rights of his wife. The problem that I have seen in many marriages is with the husband backing away from being responsible when his wife refuses to submit. When a wife does respectfully submit, a husband is much more likely to step up to the plate and be the leader she hopes and prays for. He may strike out now and then, but he is in the game. In fact they are in the game together, living out love and respect.

APPENDIX V

SEX: LOVE AND RESPECT FIRST—THEN, "JUST DO IT!"

Our Lord created sex to be holy and enjoyed. The Bible makes this clear in the Song of Solomon, which paints a picture of married love with sexual and romantic metaphors in the brightest of colors! God has never shied away from encouraging "eros" in marriage.

Although God designed sex for husbands and wives to draw closer, I have noted over many years of counseling experience that many couples clam up when the subject of sex comes up. And when I address sexuality at a marriage conference, a hush literally falls over the crowd. (It always makes me think of Christmas Eve: "Not a creature was stirring, not even a mouse!") The topic of sex makes many, if not most, people self-conscious. It is a very personal issue, which just freezes a lot of us, male or female.

Let's cut to the bedroom, where a typical "discussion" is taking place regarding sex. In one way or another, the husband is saying, "I know you want affection, but right now, I need to make love with you . . . BAD." To which the wife responds, in so many words, "(Sigh) All right, you can have your sex, but it's no fun for me, and I better get something out of it, or I'm likely to have chronic headaches."

Of course, many such discussions never get that far. She may just say "NO!" and that's the end of sex and the beginning of three days of stonewalling. Wanting (or not wanting, as the case may be) sex often leads to behavior and words that are unloving, disrespectful, manipulative, or self-serving.

It need not be.

There is a way to move forward, not necessarily to sexual nirvana, but to something that might be called "heaven on earth," at least compared to what many couples have now. How do you do it? The Love and Respect message calls on both of you to believe in the other's good will. Yes, I know you know my definition of "good will"—not really wanting to harm your mate in the long run. But sex is a short-run issue (at least for many husbands). Stick with me and I will show you how good will can help solve sexual stalemates. Here is my advice—first for husbands, then for wives:

As the husband, if you feel deprived sexually, you must not allow yourself to feel powerless and angry because you feel rejected. Instead, trust that while it doesn't seem like it, your wife does have good will toward you. Do not automatically conclude that she is disinterested in sex because she is mean-spirited and intends to punish you. Yes, she is angrily denying you at times, but this isn't necessarily the deepest desire of her heart. Realize the problem is more about her lack of sexual desire, which might be caused in part because she is hurt by how angry you have gotten when she refuses you. She may need help to reopen her heart to address her sexuality and her relationship to you, her husband. This may be the time to seek counsel from a godly, wise counselor who is competent to give you both advice about sex.

Whether or not you think a counselor is needed, this is a significant moment to let go of your negative beliefs about your wife. Her lack of sexual desire may have little to do with you. Seek her forgiveness for getting angry in the past as a way of "motivating" her to meet your sexual needs. Let her know you want to approach the problem differently, with the goal of creating mutual understanding.

As a wife, if you do have less sexual desire, one thing you should do is become aware of the message you are sending your husband: "Have eyes for me only, but don't touch me sexually—at least not very often. You can come close emotionally, but that's all. And as you stay away sexually, make sure, Buster, you stay faithful to me." What does this kind of message do to a husband? At best it hurts so deeply it can be devastating. At worst, it can drive him into another woman's waiting and willing arms.

At this point, I will make a significant qualification about what I have been saying concerning the sexual needs of men and women. So far I have pictured the husband as the one who needs sex and the wife as the one who often is not interested. I am well aware that many wives need sex more than their husbands. I have had many women tell me just that. The problem I have been addressing (he wants it; she doesn't) is what I see far more often than not. I am speaking about this subject in general terms. Twenty years of counseling experience convinces me it is safe to say, for every marriage where "the wife wants it and he doesn't," there are many more marriages where the reverse is true.

Having said this, I am insistent that couples look to (and believe) 1 Corinthians 7:3, where Paul clearly teaches that husband and wife must seek to meet each other's sexual needs. How does that happen? First, both spouses must ask, "Is it okay that God has created my mate to have a need I don't have, or at least not in the same way?" The wife must learn to ask, "Is it okay that my husband has a greater need for sex than I do?" The husband must learn to ask, "Is it okay that my wife has a greater need for affection and emotional connecting than she does for sex?"

If you both can say yes to those questions, that's a big first step toward sexual maturity. The mature husband realizes his wife has a need for affection in and of itself and he chooses to meet her need, even though he doesn't understand it completely. And the mature wife realizes that her husband did not ask to be created with an anatomy that needs sexual release on a regular basis. She chooses to meet that need, even though she does not understand it completely. Both of them realize that although God made husband and wife with needs that are equal in importance, He did not make them with needs that are the same in kind.

So far so good. Now, I have something more—something extremely important—to say to husbands. Yes, I realize you feel deprived, but a reminder is in order. If you neglect (or don't give much thought to) being close to your wife, open with your wife, understanding of your wife, at peace with your wife, loyal to your wife, or esteeming of your wife (C-O-U-P-L-E), you are shooting yourself in the foot. If you refuse her all these things I just listed to "teach her a lesson"—that she cannot deprive you sexually—you have shot yourself in the other foot. You have sent her the wrong message, and she will not hear your heart. She won't hear you trying to say, "Please respect my need for sex." All she will hear is, "I don't love you; I just want to use you." Bottom line: if you want to move forward to help your wife understand your sexual needs, you cannot deprive her of her emotional needs. By way of analogy, she cannot put her ear to your chest and listen to the deepest beat of your heart if you are figuratively screaming at the top of your lungs and banging her on the head. Some approaches just don't work.

Husbands, remember: God has designed your wife to nurture and empathize. When you share your sexual need in a reasonable, loving (and yes, respectful) way, most wives want to help. But you have to approach her humbly and honestly. You cannot mask your sexual need behind hostility and threats and expect her to decode your sexual pain. The typical good-willed wife knows her husband has this sexual need, and she isn't consciously trying to put her husband in a sex-starved state.

Then why, the husband is surely asking, do I get so little sex? In all probability, your wife isn't responding because you have not been consistently gentle and meek in this matter of sex. (For men who think "meek" is for sissies, remember Moses was called "meek" and he was no sissy [see Numbers 12:3 KJV].) In other words, you are not predictably tender with her as you share your need. Oh, you may be sweet and patient for a while, but then you explode with frustration and anger. This is the real problem: your inconsistent approach to her emotionally, which leads to the explosions. It is not her "evil will" to make you suffer. Your inconsistency sets you back each time. Patiently and consistently practice C-O-U-P-L-E and see what happens with your good-willed wife. (In fact, ask her if what I am saying is not true for her.)

Most wives want to connect emotionally and sexually with their husbands, but God did not design them to drool every time they have a thought about sex. The husband needs to see how God has designed his wife. Women are sexual beings, but there are moments during the month when they feel less sexual than others. Nonetheless, I believe the typical couple can enjoy a healthy and satisfying sexual relationship throughout most of the month, because God has created male and female to mutually satisfy each other (see 1 Corinthians 7:3).

Look at it this way: as a husband you can try to be close, open, and understanding but you won't satisfy your wife emotionally 100 percent of the time. Wives who think their husbands must satisfy their every emotional need all of the time must let go of unrealistic expectations. (For example, what man is able to discuss relationships, the needs of children, emotional feelings . . . in the same way a woman can?) The wife must let go of her dreams of what went on in Paradise before the Fall. Nonetheless, I do believe any husband can respond to his wife's emotional needs up to 80 percent of the time.

The 80 percent rule also holds for wives. A wife isn't going to "perform" sexually at the 100 percent level of a typical man's imagination. No wife is going to be available as he imagines Eve must have been available in the days before fig leaves. Nonetheless, I believe any wife can respond to her husband's needs up to 80 percent of the time. When a wife feels genuinely and consistently loved by her husband, she will respond sexually. And when a husband fails to be loving (and all husbands do from time to time), he must always remember to say, "Honey, I am truly sorry. Will you forgive me for being unloving?" When the typical wife hears that from her husband, it makes her melt, and puts her in a far better state of mind to be approached about sex.

Please know that I realize it isn't always as simple as I describe. As I talk about C-O-U-P-L-E principles I am not trying to give husbands six "new and improved sex toys" to lure their wives into bed. I am trying to give husbands pure and simple wisdom that will lead to a mutually satisfying sex life and a mutually satisfying emotional connection. Recent research in sex and marriage is bringing out some interesting information. Regarding the sex act, the traditional view has been: desire for sex leads to sexual arousal, which leads to orgasm (desire, arousal, orgasm). This sequence is still true for many. Today, however, some of the best research finds something different is true for the person with lesser sexual desire. Instead of waiting for sexual desire to surface, one chooses to enter into the act of sex and then the desire comes. This new view, which works for many, says: make a decision to have sex, which leads to arousal, which then leads to desire (sex, arousal, desire). The general idea is that desire for sex increases after one chooses to be sexual with one's spouse.

Stealing a line from the Nike commercial, sex specialists are calling on couples to "Just Do It!" Encouragingly, after "just doing it" those with lesser sexual desire are finding a wonderful change in their marriage and in improving personal sexual desires.[i]

The "Just Do It!" approach to sex reminds me of what Paul says in 1 Corinthians 7:3: "The husband must fulfill his duty to his wife, and likewise also the wife to her husband." I know the word "duty" makes it sound like sex is some kind of required obligation devoid of joy, but not so. The truth is, as we seek to do our "duty" out of love for each other and reverence for God, good things happen. It may seem like a meaningless duty to meet the emotional needs of a wife, but, oh, the pleasure this brings her! When a husband meets her needs, the typical wife in turn responds to her husband and both are happy. It may seem like a meaningless duty to meet the sexual needs of a husband, but, oh, the pleasure this brings him! When a wife meets his need, the typical husband responds to his wife and both are happy.

Again, I know it isn't always just as simple as finding some new research and a new approach, but as I say in *Love & Respect*, when it comes to conflict about sex, "the issue isn't the issue." The real issue is love for her, respect for him. Seek that together and sex will be a fantastic part of your total life as husband and wife.

---

[i] R. Basson, "Using a Different Model for Female Sexual Response to Address Women's Problematic Low Sexual Desire," *Journal of Sex and Marital Therapy*, 2001, 27:295–403.

APPENDIX VI

EMERSON'S ADDITIONAL COMMENTARY

Session 1, Question 5

Some couples think they are the only ones having trouble in their marriage and they begin to feel defeated. In the face of this trouble one of the spouses may declare: 'I married the wrong person!' Be assured that marital troubles happen to everyone, everywhere. It is what is called a 'global experience,' so no husband or wife should feel alone or abnormal when trouble, big or small, hits the marriage. Actually, knowing that millions of married couples are in the same boat can become a source of encouragement. This kind of 'negative encouragement' can actually lighten the heart.

For example, a captain may tell his crew a bad storm is coming, and while this is not positive news, it prepares his sailors to remain inwardly calm and roll with the waves. The sailors can say to themselves, "Millions of other sailors have made it through bad storms and we can too." The same truth holds for marriage. The husband and wife can say, "Millions of couples have had marital troubles and made it, and we can make it too."

For excellent advice on how to deal with trouble in your marriage, look at Paul's general instruction in Ephesians 4:26: "Be angry, and yet do not sin." Paul is recognizing anger as a normal and (in some cases) correct emotion to have. But he also puts in a note of caution. Too much anger, or the wrong kind, can be sinful. In other words, "righteous anger" can become unrighteous, especially in a marriage. Just because my wife, Sarah, gets angry with me does not mean she is sinning and that I have a bad marriage. I cannot assume that I made a mistake in marrying this woman and start thinking that another woman would appreciate me and be more understanding and romantic. It could well be her anger is justified, and I need to be repentant and teachable because God is using her to correct me. If her anger is based on a misunderstanding, I need to be patient and try to clarify the issue. Do I want to go through all this trouble? No. But is this just the kind of trouble God told me would come? Yes. Should I conclude that I married the wrong person because she is angry with me? No. Should I realize this is part and parcel of normal marriage and be encouraged? Yes! I do not rejoice in the trouble we may be having, but I continually rejoice in the hope that God will make a way where there seems to be no way.

Session 1, Question 11

How Paul uses the Greek language in Ephesians 5:33 is extremely revealing and very important. Simply stated, when he uses the Greek words for love (*agape*) and respect (*phobetai*) he puts both expressions in the imperative mood. The imperative mood always means a command is being given. Clearly, God is giving a command to both the husband and the wife. That is why the New International Version, one of the best of the newer translations, leaves no doubt. The husband "must love his wife . . . and the wife must respect her husband" (Ephesians 5:33 NIV).

Sadly, however, some have interpreted Ephesians 5:33 to mean that the wife's respect for her husband can be conditional. She need only show respect for him after she feels loved. If, in her eyes, he has not been loving enough she may feel justified in ignoring God's command to her in Ephesians 5:33b. I have had many wives tell me, "If he loves me first, I'll respect him. If he does not love me in the way I want, it is foolish to show him respect."

What is so disturbing is that these wives are not trying to be mean or willful, just honest and sincere. But they might as well take a pair of scissors and cut Ephesians 5:33b out of their Bibles. What would we think of a husband who declares, "Lord, I don't have to obey Your commands to love my wife until she is lovable and triggers feelings of love in me"? The bottom line is very clear: just as a husband is commanded to love his wife even if she is not as lovable as he would like, so a wife is commanded to respect her husband, even if he is not as loving as she wants him to be.

Session 2, Question 7

In "The Tenth Anniversary Card" story, the encoded message sent by the wife in her angry response to getting a birthday card on her anniversary was, in so many words, "If you really loved me, you wouldn't foul up like this!" When the husband responded defensively (and unlovingly), his encoded message was: "Hey, don't get so angry with me. My heart was in the right place. Your disrespect is devastating me!" (Note: the typical husband does not always think consciously about being disrespected. He probably isn't aware of his need to feel respected, or if he is consciously aware, he feels uncomfortable voicing his need to his wife. Whatever his state of mind, the point is that deep down he feels disrespect.)

In the "All You Want Me for Is Sex" story, there are several encoded messages. When the husband walks in after a week on the road, hoping for a big kiss, his wife lets fly with everything that is on her mind. She is buried in details, crises, things to be done. She needs his reassurance that he loves and understands her, and to hear "How can I help?" Instead, he feels disrespect and sends his own encoded message with a bit of sarcasm for flavor: "Great to see you after a week!" Later that night in bed, when he attempts to be sexually intimate, his wife sends a short but simple encoded message: "Don't. I'm too tired." She could have used the timeless phrase, "I have a headache," but the real message was the same: "I don't feel loved, and you aren't getting any warm, intimate responses from me!"

More encoded messages follow: he rolls away, saying nothing, but the message is there: "Disrespected again! See if I give you any loving words at all." From her female perspective, she fires another code—"You're so insensitive!"—which is once again her way of saying, "I want you to love me, not sexually at the moment, but just hold me and care about the week of misery I've just gone through!"

From there the conversation heats up and real feelings surface. From his male perspective, the husband lets his wife know he didn't appreciate not getting any kind of "Welcome home" greeting as he walked in the door. Instead he heard a litany of what sounded like complaints from a woman who seems to take for granted what he is going through for his family out there in the dog-eat-dog world. Feeling disrespected, he finally says, "Am I just a meal ticket to you?" In other words, "Don't you respect me at all?"

Feeling totally unloved, his wife unloads her frustration with another encoded message. He never asked her how she had been doing with the kids, the house, the school—*everything*. When he finally seems interested in her at all, it's for one thing. The husband is not cowed and sends his own encoded message in a short speech that lets her know he had been gone for a week (in other words, no sex for a week). He wasn't too pleased with no kiss (there were kisses once, earlier in their marriage) and being asked why he had gotten home "so early." He emphatically ends the conversation with: "Thanks. That makes my day." Another bit of sarcastic code that simply means: "I am sick of all this disrespect! What's the use?"

Session 4, Question 8

Although many husbands don't seem to "get it" about how to love their wives correctly, a wife must ask herself three questions: "Is his heart in the right place? Am I judging him too severely? Could the real problem be my lack of genuine respect for him?" One wife wrote to tell me:

"My husband left me and refused to take my calls or pleas. He tried to love me for twenty-one years and finally my facial expressions, tones, and negative disrespectful behavior became too much for him to bear. He broke and told me I was mean and he was not going to let me treat him like that again. I was devastated and hounded him for months. . . . I didn't know the damage I had already done the first month we were married [when I] removed my wedding ring and spat in his face, and many, many episodes after that for twenty more years."

This woman's letter is heartbreaking. The guy tried to love her for twenty-one years. He did "get it," but her disrespect sent the message, "You don't get it, stupid," and it defeated him. This story graphically illustrates a key truth, which is framed best in this question: even if my spouse isn't "getting it" as perfectly as I would like, will it help to criticize or to encourage him or her?

Session 4, Question 14

When a wife comes across as disrespectful to her husband, she thinks it's like a "wet noodle" across her husband's face, just annoying enough to get his attention and hear her real message: "I'm hurting. Please reassure me that you understand, value, and love me." But if a man used the same kind of disrespect toward another man, it would be like a brick in the face! He can think of few men, if any, who talk to him in this way. Difficult as it may be at times, the man of honor must decode his wife's words (which could be hitting as hard as any brick) and hear her real message, asking for his love.

Session 6, Question 14

Concerning answer *b*: don't worry, there will be plenty to talk about, and as I say on page 153 of *Love & Respect*, husbands can just mostly listen.

Concerning answer *c*: don't let the "urgent" things that fill your day squeeze out the truly important. Understanding a wife means talking to a wife; you can find the time if you really want to. Sarah and I did.

Concerning answer *d*: of course understanding takes feelings, especially feelings of empathy. But to know what and how to feel, spouses need to talk. You and your spouse may want to schedule regular time to talk. For some couples, twenty minutes every evening is satisfactory. For others, an evening dinner or Saturday morning breakfast once a week works best. Work out your own schedule. The point is that talking is the means, understanding is the end.

Session 7, Question 4

The more I studied Scripture, the more I saw 1 Corinthians 7:3–5 as a great illustration of how marriages can have trouble—actually trouble ordained by God, because He has wired male and female so differently. We might say that because God made you male and female, He created you to have conflict and intends that the two of you use the conflict to deepen your mutual understanding of one another. Is this fun to go through? No, it isn't, but you can trust that it is His will. Because you have conflict you are not outside of God's will, nor did you marry the wrong person. (See again 1 Corinthians 7:28!)

In 1 Corinthians 7:3–5, God lays down a basic truth for spouses: neither spouse has total authority over his or her body in the sexual area, because the other spouse has authority as well. Since Scripture gives both spouses "equal power" in making a sexual decision, they can and must work together to find a solution. So, how would a couple work out a possible conflict about having sex tonight as mentioned in the question above?

To those spouses studying this question together, I urge you to read page 158 of *Love & Respect* carefully, perhaps more than once. These paragraphs contain the "solution" to marital conflict.

Session 10, Question 3

Obviously, for biblical hierarchy to be lived out in a love and respect fashion, it is necessary for a husband to operate from an attitude of good will—never wishing his wife and children any harm. But a good-willed man can be stubborn, proud, and prone to poor judgment from time to time. Being good-willed does not guarantee perfect, or even competent, behavior on every occasion. Being the "head" is a difficult task, and a husband needs all the help he can get. Ideally, a wife is his willing helpmeet and he is willing to listen to her suggestions. If he resists her suggestions, another approach for the wife to take is Peter's advice to enter quietness (see 1 Peter 3:1–4). This does not mean giving him the cold shoulder or pouting. It does mean withholding comments and criticisms, even though the wife is sure that what she has to say has much merit.

Withholding her comments can be extremely difficult for the typical wife who believes talking is the way to solve problems. One "extremely verbal" spouse had a husband who let her handle the money, then later he would criticize her for "doing it all wrong." She tried to get him to talk about it (so she could argue her side vehemently), but he could never "find the right time." Finally, with great difficulty, she tried just "being quiet," and it worked! Slowly he changed, and the wife eventually wrote to me: "We are doing very, very well. My husband is transforming before my eyes. My being silent . . . [has] become a habit and I'll eat my words, or choose my timing, or . . . just let it go . . . [and] now my husband has become a leader. A man that's [sic] easy to admire and respect . . . and love."

"Just being quiet" seems counterintuitive to many wives. They wonder how anything can be decided if there is no talking. God's answer through 1 Peter 3:1 is: ". . . without a word. . . ." To a woman, this is absurd. Therefore, she must take God's word for it by faith and use respectful silence for a season of time to try to break a husband's bad habits and disobedience of God's call to love his wife. Many wives have told me how well it works to use respectful silence on a good-willed husband. Remember, "good-willed" means that a husband means no harm in the ultimate sense, even though in the "immediate now" he can be acting pretty badly. What a verbal and aggressive wife must remember is that her husband may be acting badly due to his fear of her verbal skills and disrespect. Silence on her part gives him a chance to deal with her on more even terms. That is when he will let down his defenses and quite possibly change, as the husband described above changed.

Session 10, Question 11

So, how does mutual-submission-even-though-the-husband-has-final-responsibility-and-authority work out in the daily stuff of life? If there is an honest stalemate between husband and wife that threatens to cause a real rift, the wife is called upon to submit to her husband. For example, a *Love & Respect* couple has a serious disagreement over homeschooling versus sending a child to a public school or a private Christian school with high tuition. A decision must be made by September. Suppose they discuss this thoroughly as he tries in every way to show her love and she tries to show respect. Finally, all alternatives are exhausted, and they still strongly disagree. Because of some serious financial problems at present, and because he has checked the public school out and it gets a decent academic rating, the husband decides that this year at least the child goes to public school. His wife is not happy, but she is called to defer to her husband. She is not called to agree with him, and in the long run her position may prove to be the better one, necessitating a change of course. Nonetheless, because the husband has been given the greater responsibility, he must have the greater authority. So for now, the child will attend the public school even though the wife believes it will be at the expense of the child's spiritual welfare.

Secular culture says that such a decision is unfair to the wife, and in a sense that is true. However—and this is an extremely important point—would it be more unfair to the husband to hold him primarily responsible for the marriage and the family and not give him final authority? For a wife to say, "You can't do that, we're equal!" means she grabs veto power. Few things feel so unfair and dishonoring to a husband as that.

Egalitarians take the position that a husband and wife should make a decision based on who has the greatest expertise. But that begs the question, what do you do when both spouses claim to have greater insight? Coming back to our home school or public school debate, that was precisely the case. Neither one would give an inch. A couple may seldom come to an impasse like this, but they should have a theological and organizational understanding in place in the event there is the need for a tiebreaker decision. This idea may sound ridiculous to those who dream of a perfect egalitarian world, but it makes perfect sense to the couple who wants to make the institution of marriage work long-term. In a Christian marriage a woman does not have the biblical right to say, "I'm going to do what I prefer in spite of my husband's opinion. I feel I'm right. This is the twenty-first century! Besides, I make more money than he does." That is not what Scripture plainly teaches. The woman is not the head; for better or worse, the man has that responsibility.

Does making the man the head always result in perfect decisions? Obviously not. We live in a fallen world, and husbands are quite fallible. Nonetheless the biblical model for decision-making in the marriage is better than the two alternatives: (1) the wife is in charge; (2) both are in charge. Egalitarianism sounds like it might be more fair, but there is no answer for the honest stalemate, and it often fosters exhausting negotiation or such strict boundaries concerning "who has authority over what" that spiritual oneness is undermined and eroded.

Session 10, Question 12

All of the quotes from pages 221–222 in *Love & Respect* center around what I call Leadership 101—the most basic of all leadership principles: if you give somebody primary responsibility they must have primary authority to carry out that responsibility. One way of looking at Leadership 101 is described in choice *b*. If the husband has 51 percent of the responsibility, he must have 51 percent of the authority. But ranking herself under her husband's responsibility and authority is a choice each wife must make for herself. According to Ephesians 5:22, she does this out of love and reverence for Christ: "Place yourselves under your husband's authority as you have placed yourself under the Lord's authority" (translation mine).

To violate Leadership 101 is to frustrate a husband. He may get angry and dictatorial or he can rebel by becoming Mr. Passive and deserting his God-given responsibility, allowing his wife to be head. During many years of counseling, I have seen both kinds of husbands and neither approach leads to a happy marriage. I am not saying all this is easy, especially for the wife who is capable, verbal, and aggressive. But allowing the husband to be head pays off in the long run, as one wife discovered. She and her husband are both professors at a major American university. Recently, they had one of their few major stalemates. The decision involved purchasing a vacation home. She wanted it, but he did not, for financial reasons. Rather than yielding to her husband's authority she insisted that they do things her way. Her letter continues:

"Until the vacation home stalemate, we had been conscious to not live a lifestyle that was dependent on my income. [But] I wanted a vacation home and pushed the point, even though my husband didn't support the purchase. Turning this decision back to my husband was one of the first things I did after reading your book. Apart from the fact that I violated my husband's authority, I also realized that the 'issue wasn't the issue' and that purchasing something we couldn't afford on my husband's income was inconsistent with a commitment to honor his desire to provide for me and felt very disrespectful to him."

With no regrets, this wife told her husband she would support whatever he decided to do with the vacation condo. After telling her how critically important it was to him that she had stepped back and allowed him to be the leader, he decided to sell the condo sometime in the future. What surprised her the most, however, was how right it felt to respect her husband's authority. She had feared being stripped of her dignity; instead all she lost was her initial sense of contentiousness.

Session 11, Question 4

What I say here is for good-willed wives and good-willed husbands who are willing to practice Love and Respect as they discuss a problem that affects the entire family. The wife should keep in mind that her husband may be more open to feedback and suggestions than she first thought. And the husband should remember that spiritual leadership is his responsibility.[i] As a husband, realize that spiritual leadership is not rocket science; it is more of an art that you can master if you are willing to do three things:

a. Show your wife that Christ is an important part of your life: pray and read Scripture on your own and with her; talk together about what Scripture means in your lives; pray together for guidance in parenting and in being a Love and Respect couple who want to honor the Lord.

b. Be there, part of whatever is going on—family devotions, praying before bed, going to church, and other spiritual endeavors. If you are not as verbal as your wife, delegate certain duties (like the Bible story) to her. Leaders delegate all the time; it is part of being a leader. Your job is be sure everyone is listening as they see that you are interested and "into" what is happening.

c. As you make decisions, from small ones to big ones, make it clear to your wife and children that you are depending on Christ for wisdom. Make Proverbs 3:5–6 a family motto. Once or twice a week, as your wife may share a concern about one of the children, or some other problem, stop right there and lead in a short prayer about the situation. Take the issue that may be burdening your wife and carry it up to God. You don't have to solve her problem; give it to the One who can solve it. This will mean more than the world to your wife.

[i] The husband's responsibility for spiritual leadership is strongly implied in Ephesians 5:23–27. Note especially v. 23: "For the husband is the head of the wife, as Christ also is the head of the church." The parallel is clear: because Jesus Christ is the responsible spiritual leader of the church, so a husband is to be the responsible spiritual leader in relationship to his wife.

In short, to be a spiritual leader the husband needs to show up and be interested. And, just as important, his wife needs to step back a bit if necessary and let him lead. He may be halting, unsure, a bit clumsy at times, but he can do it if given a chance. If a wife undercuts, criticizes, shows disapproval because all is not being done as well as she thinks it should be done, the husband will sense this in an instant and back off. A leader needs followers. A husband's wife should be his most supportive and enthused follower.

Session 13, Question 3

That you may be suffering right now, I have no doubt. But have you considered that God is allowing this suffering in order to reward you? The writer of Hebrews instructs us to fix "our eyes on Jesus, the author and perfecter of faith, who for the joy set before Him endured the cross, despising the shame, and has sat down at the right hand of the throne of God" (Hebrews 12:2). When I began teaching people in deeply troubled marriages that their present suffering would be rewarded in heaven, I thought they would turn me off. Instead, I found many of them saying things like, "I never thought about God using my spouse in my life," or "This gives me a desire to endure since what I do matters to God." Following are some typical letters:

"One question I was asking God was, 'How can someone you love so much be so hurtful and just turn their back on you?' I was feeling really let down and pushed away. . . . [But God's] answer to me was: 'I've been there, I know how you feel and I died for you.' Oh my, what a revelation! This was not an issue of whether my [spouse] was treating me correctly, but whether I was looking at this whole relationship the way God does. [My suffering] is a form of worship, obedience and praise to God. . . . That is a tall order to meet, but what a joy to know I am doing it all for the glory of God."

"I have been married for 37 years . . . What an eye opener for me that I should be loving and respectful, not for my [spouse], but for God."

"Even if I see no change in my marriage, I know I am doing what pleases God and this alone gives me peace and takes the edge off the hurt and pain. The emotions are less and less significant and there is hope. When I fail, I just thank God for His mercy and patience."

FOCUS ON THE FAMILY®

Welcome to the Family!

Whether you received this book as a gift, borrowed it, or purchased it yourself, we're glad you read it. It's just one of the many helpful, insightful, and encouraging resources produced by Focus on the Family.

In fact, that's what Focus on the Family is all about—providing inspiration, information, and biblically based advice to people in all stages of life.

It began in 1977 with the vision of one man, Dr. James Dobson, a licensed psychologist and author of 18 best-selling books on marriage, parenting, and family. Alarmed by the societal, political, and economic pressures that were threatening the existence of the American family, Dr. Dobson founded Focus on the Family with one employee and a once-a-week radio broadcast aired on only 36 stations.

Now an international organization, the ministry is dedicated to preserving Judeo-Christian values and strengthening and encouraging families through the life-changing message of Jesus Christ. Focus ministries reach families worldwide through 10 separate radio broadcasts, two television news features, 13 publications, 18 Web sites, and a steady series of books and award-winning films and videos for people of all ages and interests.

• • •

For more information about the ministry, or if we can be of help to your family, simply write to Focus on the Family, Colorado Springs, CO 80995 or call (800) A-FAMILY (232-6459). Friends in Canada may write Focus on the Family, P.O. Box 9800, Stn. Terminal, Vancouver, B.C. V6B 4G3 or call (800) 661-9800. Visit our Web site—www.family.org—to learn more about Focus on the Family or to find out if there is an associate office in your country.

We'd love to hear from you!

www.loveandrespect.com

- **Locate** Live Conferences
- **View** Streaming Video and Audio
- **Chat** with Emerson
- **Read** Articles and Testimonials
- **Find** DVDs, CDs and Books

E-mail Us Your Story!

Please give us the privilege of hearing how the
Love and Respect message has impacted you,
your marriage, or a loved one. E-mail Emerson at:

story@loveandrespect.com

Love and Respect Ministries Inc. is a non-profit organization, 501(c)(3),
formed to conduct conferences that instruct husbands and wives regarding
how to build strong marriage relationships.